Ki

A Practical Guide
for Westerners

William Reed

Japan Publications, Inc.

Published by JAPAN PUBLICATIONS, INC., Tokyo and New York
Distributors:
UNITED STATES: *Kodansha America, Inc., through Farrar, Straus & Giraux, 19 Union Square West, New York, 10003.* CANADA: *Fitzhenry & Whiteside Ltd., 195 Allstate Parkway, Markham, Ontario, L3R 4T8.* BRITISH ISLES AND EUROPEAN CONTINENT: *Premier Book Marketing Ltd., 1 Gower Street, London WC1E 6HA.* AUSTRALIA AND NEW ZEALAND: *Bookwise International, 54 Crittenden Road, Findon, South Australia 5023.* THE FAR EAST AND JAPAN: *Japan Publications Trading Co., Ltd., 1–2–1, Sarugaku-cho, Chiyoda-ku, Tokyo 101.*

First edition: June 1986
Fourth printing: September 1993

LCCC No. 85–081367
ISBN 0–87040–640–X

Printed in U.S.A.

To Leah, Adria, and Benjamin . . .
that they may learn from my mistakes.

Foreword

At the close of the Second World War, few people could have imagined that Japan would ever revive from the devastation. Life itself existed on a subsistence level, and the economy lay in ruins. Forty years later, Japan had astonished the world with its miraculous recovery.

Much of the world was also surprised that the Japanese, small in stature, a tiny nation with limited resources, could take on the world in combat; and despite their defeat, recuperate so completely within a few decades.

While it is true that Japan was treated very favorably after the war, historically the Japanese nation has been able to muster the power to survive in a crisis. Seeking to know the source of this power, an increasing number of thoughtful foreigners have sought answers in the study of Zen, the Tea Ceremony, or the Martial Arts. In their study, they have begun important research on the quiet strength that characterizes much of the culture of traditional Japan. Mr. Reed is one of these people.

Mr. Reed originally came to Japan in 1972, when he began his study of the Japanese language at Waseda University in Tokyo. At the same time he began his study of Ki and Aikidô, and of Japanese culture. His return to the United States in 1973 coincided with the beginnings of the rapid spread of Aikidô schools abroad, just two years after I founded the Ki Society International.

I introduced Aikidô to America for the first time in 1953. Beginning in Hawaii, Aikidô schools were soon established in over 20 states, and eventually spread to the entire country; as well as to many other countries in the world.

Aikidô is a way of learning to live in harmony with the Ki of the Universe. I taught Aikidô as such, but was gradually saddened by the fact that most people saw and practiced only the Aikidô techniques alone, completely ignoring the essence of Ki.

Mr. Reed began his study with Aikidô, but he saw in it the essence of Ki. Furthermore, he saw in Ki the fundamental basis for much of Japanese thought and culture. Consumed by a desire to pursue this study in depth, he returned to Japan in 1983, and entered my school for Aikidô instructors.

Mr. Reed has pursued this study with thoroughness and intelligence. Fluent in both reading and speaking Japanese, he surprised me by pointing out translation errors in Japanese-English dictionaries and College entrance examination questions. Using his bilingual ability, he was able to discover errors in many books written in English about Japanese culture. Furthermore, he was surprised to find how few of the Japanese themselves were aware of or appreciated the spiritual depth of their own heritage. Mr. Reed came to Japan and gained direct access to many genuine elements of this heritage. This book is a result of his efforts to introduce Ki, the spirit of Japanese culture, to the West. It is a considerable achievement; a fair and sincere presentation of the universal aspects of the Japanese spirit.

Tokyo, 1985

KÔICHI TÔHEI

10th degree Black Belt-Aikidô
Founder: Ki Society International;
Shin Shin Tôitsu Aikidô, and Kiatsu Therapy

Preface

We are born into the world, and in most cases we leave it through no choice of our own. The human mind and body are both fraught with limitations and blessed with potential. Whether we thrive, or merely survive in life, depends on how well we develop our capacity to cope in a crisis. Whether physical, mental, or emotional, every crisis is rich with possibilities for both danger and opportunity. Every crisis is a test of intelligence; not of what you know, but of how you act when you don't know. The outcome depends on our attitude. It requires imagination and energy to grasp the opportunity in a crisis. That force within us which gives us initiative, which drives and inspires us to overcome obstacles, is *Ki*.

But for most people, Ki is a flickering flame; sometimes asserting itself, sometimes faltering. This unsteadiness produces a vague and free-floating anxiety, as if something bad might happen. As long as Ki is weak, this diffuse feeling of dread will continue. Eventually such a person will come to see himself as a victim in life. The victim mentality focuses on limitations, and ignores possibilities. Always avoiding problems, the victim can never avoid stress. Anxiety cannot be dealt with on its own terms. Neither drugs, relaxation, nor meditation will take it away, because most of these methods seek to protect the flame rather than strengthen it.

Methods for training and developing strong Ki have a long history in Japan. Highly refined and practical techniques have evolved for developing the human spirit, through disciplines which provide dangerous opportunities. Whether in calligraphy, martial arts training, or the performing arts, students are presented with a graded series of dilemmas and practical problems which are beyond the present capacity of the student to solve. The frustration which builds leads the student to a crisis. By way of example, philosophical principles, and strong spirit, the master leads the student to discover the way to solve the problem and surpass himself. Solving the problem awakens the mind; broadening peripheral awareness and sharpening intuition. The result is an increase in intelligence; an improved ability to respond to problems. With practice, this ability carries over into daily life.

Though many of these Ways, or disciplines, have received a lot of attention in the West, their interpretation has been considerably distorted by people whose experience in the arts, and Japanese language ability, is very limited. As a result, Ki has remained an Oriental mystery, rather than becoming a practical force that we can use in our daily lives. This book is an attempt to clarify the misconceptions surrounding Ki; to explain how to develop Ki; illustrate how Ki is trained and expressed in some of the Japanese arts; and to offer practical suggestions for using Ki to solve problems in daily life.

Acknowledgments

Blessings are sometimes born of misfortune; strength, of adversity. Life arranges connections and affinities for us that we can scarcely understand at the time. When Kôichi Tôhei brought Aikidô to America for the first time in February of 1953, I was barely 6 months old. My first encounter with Master Tôhei was at the age of 12, through a book on Aikidô and self-defense, which I purchased in desperation, after being badly bullied on the way home from school. Eight years later, quite by accident I discovered that book again and determined to go to Japan and study directly with Master Tôhei. That decision changed my life, leading me to spend a number of years in Japan.

Everything from the Ki principles and Ki exercises, to specific insights and encouragement to study Ki in Japanese culture, I owe to Master Tôhei. His genius has made sense of a great Oriental heritage. His hard work and lifelong devotion to teaching Ki has made it available to people in many countries of the world.

The Ki exercises presented in this book represent only a small portion of those which Master Tôhei has developed for the Ki Society curriculum. Those interested in a serious study of Ki should make reference to books published by the Ki Society, listed in the Bibliography; and should seek instruction from certified instructors at one of the Ki-no-Kenkyû-Kai schools, also listed under sources of further reference.

I owe a second debt of gratitude to Hal and Marilyn Shook, of the Life Management Services, Inc., in McLean, Virginia, for their enlightened and practical career counseling. Their inspiration and guidance gave me the courage to pursue the path of my own choosing.

Special thanks go to Dan and Jackie DeProspero, without whose friendship, photography, and modeling skills, most of the illustrations in this book would not have been possible. Also appearing in the photographs are Eric Martin, Julie Leidig, and Kumi Tsuboi.

For countless hours of Aikidô instruction and personal advice, I would like to thank Mr. Koretoshi Maruyama, Mr. Yutaka Ôtsuka, and Mr. Taketoshi Kataoka of the Aikidô Instructor's school; and Mr. George Simcox, chief instructor of the Virginia Ki Society. For close personal guidance in *Shodô* practice, I would like to thank my teacher, Mr. Hiroshi Morioka, who also did the calligraphy for the cover. For special editorial advice and modeling for the *Noh* chapter, I would like to thank Rick Emmert of the Noh Research Archives, and David Crandall of the Hôsho School of *Noh*; and for the Tea Ceremony, Jackie DeProspero. All calligraphy, unless otherwise specified, was done by the author.

Credits for specific photographs are as follows:

Yamaoka Tesshû's signatures, and their microscopic analysis, were made possible by Professor Katsujô Terayama and Professor John Stevens; reproduced by permission from *Zen and the Art of Calligraphy* (by Sôgen Ômori and Katsujô Terayama, translated by John Stevens, Routledge and Kegan Paul, London, 1983).

Tea Ceremony photographs appearing in figures: 10-31, 10-32, 10-33, 10-34, 10-37, 10-39, and 10-46 were reprinted with permission of the Tankôsha Publishing Company, Kyôto.

The *Noh* pictures appearing in figures: 9-4, 9-24, and 9-27 were furnished courtesy of Mitsu Takahashi. Those in figures: 9-6, 9-10, 9-17, 9-18, 9-20, 9-37, 9-38, 9-39, and 9-40 were supplied by David Crandall, and taken by Kunihei Kameda. Special thanks goes to Mr. Shôzo Masuda of the Noh Research Archives for his permission to reprint the photographs in figures: 9-5, 9-9, 9-19, 9-25, 9-33, 9-34, 9-35, and 9-36. The remainder of the *Noh* photographs were taken by Hideo Nishitani.

Most of the photographs in the book were taken by Mr. Dan DeProspero.

The mandala showing Jung's analysis of personality types (Fig. 13-1) was reprinted with permission of consultant Eleanor Corlett.

Special recognition should also be given to Mr. Iwao Yoshizaki, the President of Japan Publications, for his considerable skills in managing the project; and to Kumi Tsuboi, for her generous assistance and encouragement in interpreting certain aspects of Japanese culture.

The author would also like to acknowledge personal responsibility for any misleading statements and possible errors in the interpretation of Ki principles and Japanese culture. Entire books have been written about any one of the topics taken up in this introductory guide, by people with far more years of experience than myself. It is hoped that the reader will take this book as a starting point in conducting his or her own research, and not as a final statement on the subject. If, in conducting this research, the reader comes across conflicting opinions or interpretations, each is best considered for its own merits.

WILLIAM REED
Tokyo, December 1985

Contents

Author's Note

Throughout the book, to avoid awkward sentence construction, I have chosen masculine pronouns to describe people's actions. The term *Man* has also appeared in reference to humankind. This choice was made as an unavoidable convention in writing; no sexist implications were intended.

Westerners were deliberately selected in modeling the photographs, to suggest that Ki is not a special privileged field of study for Japanese alone. People have traditionally assumed that to master any one of the Japanese arts requires a lifetime of study, devoted to little else. Were this true, the arts would have little relevance to modern Western people. A more realistic view has it, that while one can make dramatic progress with a good teacher in a few years of part-time study, twenty years later one can still make dramatic progress in the same art.

Guide to Pronouncing Japanese Words

I was once asked by an American who saw the word, "AIKIDÔ" for the first time: "What is, **A** one **K** one **do**?" He was perfectly serious. Increased exchanges with Japan in a number of fields have brought more and more Japanese words into circulation in Western languages. With a few guidelines, you can avoid embarrassment over a mispronounced word.

a as in c*a*lm
i as in *east*
u as in *Zulu*, or p*u*ll
e as in *e*xtra, or n*e*t
o as in s*o*lo

Pay attention to the difference between long (**ô**) and short (**o**) vowels, as they can change the meaning of a word entirely. Double consonants are spoken with a slight pause in-between: *ippai* is pronounced ip-pai. There are many other rules, but these will make your words understandable to a native Japanese. Precise pronunciation is more important than you may imagine. Otherwise, though you may mean to say that you are studying *Shodô* (Brush Calligraphy), and are interested in *Go* (an ancient board game of strategy); if you mispronounce the words, you may wind up telling someone that you are studying "Jyadô" (black magic) and are interested in "Gô" (torture).

PART **I**

How to Develop
Ki

1. Mind and Body Unity

Defining Ki

A Japanese dictionary defines *Ki* (氣) as mind, spirit, or heart. It lists hundreds of expressions which use the word Ki; most of them ordinary ways of talking about human moods, attitudes, or character. It is sometimes given a more philosophical meaning. In the martial arts and Oriental medicine, the word Ki refers to a subtle form of vital energy. Ki is the life force; a source of internal strength. Like the words Zen and *Satori*, Ki has recently come into common use in Western languages. But though many books have been written in English on Zen, only a few books have addressed the subject of Ki. Deep concepts resist definition. Yet better definitions alone are no substitute for direct experience in achieving a better understanding of Ki.

The word Ki comes from the original Chinese concept of *Chi* or *Qi*, introduced to the West through acupuncture and the Chinese martial art of T'ai Chi Ch'uan. But the ancient Chinese way of thinking about life is so alien to our own, that it may not serve as the best reference in the study of Ki. Ideas are not more reliable simply because they are ancient.

Some researchers have attempted to appease the demands of the modern intellect for tangible evidence of the unseen. Infrared photography, and pictures taken in a high-frequency magnetic field seem to reveal a picture of the human aura. Patterns of skin resistance to low voltage electricity seem to follow the meridians mapped out by acupuncturists to show the direction of Ki flow. But none of this research has really stirred the scientific community. Early Western philosophers attempted unsuccessfully to mathematically prove the existence of God. However the mind has always eluded attempts to search for and define its essence.

It is much easier to demonstrate Ki than to try to measure or contain it. Ki operates according to definite principles. Its operation leaves physical traces, which can be easily recognized. These principles, and their operation in the human body, will be explained in this and the following chapters. For the sake of clarity, here is an operational definition:

> *Ki is a universal energy, capable of infinite expansion and contraction, which can be directed, but not contained by the mind.*

Ki cannot be directly perceived with the senses or measured by a machine. However, Ki is not merely a concept. It is a real force which can be intuitively perceived and mentally directed. Though we live in and depend on the air we breathe, we rarely notice it or appreciate its importance. Like air and water, Ki is the very source of our vitality. It is the mysterious quality which distinguishes a healthy person from a sick one; one living from one dead.

Our Ki becomes weak when we fail to understand its original nature. Though every shred of scientific evidence points to the unity of mind and body, we act as though they were separate. The old philosophical notion, of Man as a ghost in a machine, may have gone out of fashion; but we still say that we "have a head-ache," and "drag ourselves out of bed," as though it were literally true. The best way to strengthen Ki is to understand and practice the unity of mind and body.

The Four Basic Principles of Mind and Body Unification

The mind and body are not exactly the same; nor are they entirely different. Changes in blood chemistry affect consciousness; and changes in attitude affect health. The body is the visible portion of the mind. When we look at a tree, we usually forget that half of it is below the ground. Problems begin when we learn to accept as real only that which is obvious.

The shape of the shadow cast by an object depends on the direction from which it is illuminated. The four principles which follow, offer two mental and two physical perspectives on Ki. These principles, and all of the other principles in this book directly related to Ki, were developed by Master Kôichi Tôhei.

1. *Calm and Focus the Mind at the One Point in the Lower Abdomen:* The point of focus for the mind is called the One Point. On the average person, it is located roughly 10 cm (4 inches) below the navel. However this point has no definable size or position. Its position shifts farther down, and even out of the body, when-ever the upper body bends forward or leans back. Like the lowest point in a strong whirlpool, it funnels Ki in from the universe. Because Ki is capable of infinite expansion or contraction, the One Point acts like a miniature star; radiating Ki out or absorbing it in from all directions. The Ki exercises which follow make it possible to experience the One Point; but for now, consider it as a dynamic point of mental focus.

2. *Completely Release All Stress from the Body:* Complete relaxation should not result in a flaccid or collapsed state. Incorrect forms of relaxation involve only the larger muscle groups; resulting in a collapsed state in which the organs and blood vessels suffer under the unsupported weight of the upper body. It is impos-sible to develop strong Ki in this state. However releasing stress from the body makes it light and buoyant; free from unnecessary tension or restriction.

3. *Let the Weight of Every Part of the Body Settle Naturally at its Lowest Point:*
Gravity naturally keeps the weight of any object underside, without any help from

us. The lowest point of an object at rest is on the bottom of that object. However, for a moving object the lowest point is not a fixed location. A golf ball trapped inside a rolling beach ball will roll freely in response to both gravity and centrifugal force. If we resist the natural disposition of weight in our own bodily movement, our weight will come upperside; resulting in a loss of stability, and in extreme cases, dizziness.

4. Extend Ki: Ki is free like the wind. It expands and fills space in all directions. It responds to our mental direction, but is impossible to contain. Physical objects present no barrier to Ki, yet it has the power to move them. Ki seems to accelerate and flow more powerfully at certain points in the body: the eyes, the fingertips, the One Point. Because Ki travels freely, like light, to the ends of the universe, we are only aware of it as it passes through us.

These four principles are the foundation of all Ki training. Principles 1 and 4, dealing with the One Point and Ki, describe the operation of the mind. Without shape, form, or physical restriction, the mind can be used freely and powerfully. Only imagination limits its potential. Ki is quicker than the hand or eye; quicker than the mouth. But strong Ki is present only in a calm mind. A spinning top appears motionless when it whirls the fastest.

Principles 2 and 3, concerning relaxation and weight underside, describe the operation of the body. Physical laws limit the strength and development of the body. But a living body is more than a mere object; it is infused with mind and responds to Ki. The limitations of the body are largely set in the mind. Strong Ki resides in a body which is relaxed and settled, but buoyant.

Four principles, four ways of viewing the same thing; the state of mind and body unity. To understand one of them, is to know the other three. To lose one of them is to lose them all. The test of a theory is its usefulness. Though Ki cannot be directly perceived with the senses or measured with a machine, it can be experienced, tested, and strengthened. The body is the visible portion of the mind. Through the body we can know the mind. The stability, strength, and freedom of movement of the body under pressure are measures of the mind. A Ki test is a controlled application of pressure or restraint, designed to provide a form of biofeedback on the quality and depth of mind and body unity. Each test helps the student to internalize the sense of Ki. In time, the student learns to recognize Ki with or without the Ki test. The person giving the Ki test may feel challenged to see just how strong his partner has become; but it is a test, not a contest. Ki tests have the dual purpose of measuring and developing Ki.

The most effective way to develop Ki is to compare the way the body behaves with and without Ki. All of us have unconsciously developed bad habits of posture and movement. Somehow we fail to recognize how these habits gradually age and fatigue us; weakening our Ki with each day we grow older. As the flame of our Ki flickers and weakens, the body shows it with excess tension or slackness. Ki tests objectively compare the weakness and instability of our usual way of standing, sitting, or moving, with the strength of the mind and body unified. Though the contrast is obvious, it takes time to gradually change the subconscious mind. Daily Ki training is a form of spiritual and physical fine tuning; bringing us back to our original and natural state of mind-body unity.

The real benefits of Ki testing are found in correct performance and repetition. It is satisfying to pass a Ki test, but should not become a source of pride. The state of mind and body unity can just as easily be lost in the next moment. It must be continually rediscovered. Ki tests should be performed according to the ability of the student. It is impossible to fully graduate from all of the Ki tests, because they are subtle, easily forgotten, and contain many levels of difficulty. Much depends on how the test is performed. The purpose of Ki testing is to teach Ki principles, not to establish superiority or prove who is stronger. There is as much to learn in testing as there is in being tested, so partners take turns doing the tests, and help each other to learn. Lastly, the tests are not an end in themselves, but point to something much greater. Their ultimate purpose is to help both partners to learn how to coordinate mind and body, and extend Ki in whatever one does. This process opens the mind and strengthens the body; enabling us to realize our full human potential.

How to Correct Your Standing Posture

Spend just ten minutes watching people stand in line, and you will be convinced that most people don't know how to stand. Shoulders slump; arms alternately cross and dangle. Hands find no comfortable resting place. People shift their weight back and forth, not really knowing what to do with their bodies. The human body is well designed to stand erect, so standing in line shouldn't be as hard as most people make it look.

Raising the heels off of the grounds, stand on the balls of the feet, with feet at shoulder width and arms hanging freely at your sides (Fig. 1-1). Eyes should face forward, and the upper body be kept as relaxed as possible. If it is difficult to maintain balance in this position, then there is probably too much tension in the upper body. If the arch of the foot is weak, it may be difficult to maintain this position; but a healthy individual should easily be able to stand balanced like this for more than a minute. This exercise is best done barefoot.

Standing balanced on the toes not only corrects your posture, but it quickly unifies your mind and body. While the weight of the entire body falls on the balls of the feet; the weight of the upper body falls on the One Point. As long as you keep your balance, stress is released from the body, and the weight of each part settles to the lowest point. Be sure that the eyes face forward, as this keeps the head in the proper position. It is very easy to extend Ki in the correct posture. Have your partner lift straight up on your ankle, without twisting your leg; in the direction of your One Point (Fig. 1-2). Don't shift your weight or change anything about your posture to compensate for the test. Just as it is, the ankle should feel very heavy to your partner, as if it were rooted to the ground. This feeling has

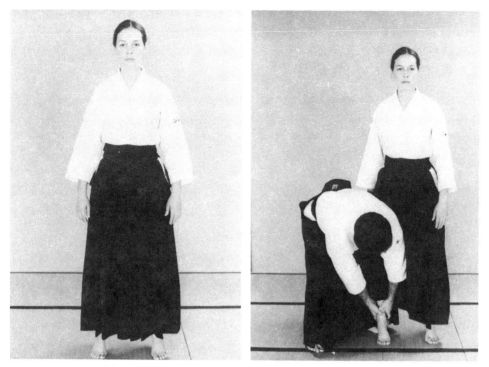

Fig. 1-1

Fig. 1-2

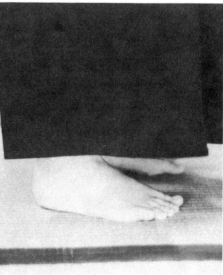

Fig. 1-3

Fig. 1-4

nothing to do with body weight or your partner's strength. You may be so stable, that you feel that your partner is not testing very hard. This stability occurs without any special effort or weight shift on your part. However the test is meaningless if your partner tries to unbalance you by pulling your leg out to the side, or leaning his body weight against your leg.

To really understand how stable this position is, the test should be repeated on the same posture, while deliberately violating one or more of the four basic principles. Even though you stand on the balls of your feet, if you look down, tense your shoulders, clench your fists, or shift your weight to either side, your partner will have no trouble lifting either ankle (Fig. 1-3). For the test to be fair, it should be performed in the same direction, with the same amount of strength. It is not a question of which is better; there is no comparison. If the test is treated as a contest or display of strength, then your partner will be tempted to use many times more strength in testing the correct posture. This is acceptable, as long as it is recognized as a harder test, and as long as the ankle is not pulled sideways or twisted.

Putting unnecessary tension in the body violates the principles of mind and body unity. Therefore it robs us of stability and internal strength. Yet inadvertently, this is what we do whenever we slip into a dark or depressed mood. Our posture reflects our mental state as faithfully as a mirror reflects our face; clearly signaling our attitude to other people. Worse still, it reinforces itself each time we fail to correct it.

Putting the weight on the balls of the feet centers the body, takes the weight off of the heels, and gently stretches the lower spine. Stretching is designed to adjust the body, and return it to a natural posture, not to be maintained indefinitely. If you lower your heels so that they barely touch the ground, you can maintain this posture comfortably for long periods of time. There is no need to fidget, fold the arms, or stand with hands in your pockets. Though the heels lightly touch the ground, the weight will fall on the balls of the feet (Fig. 1-4). This posture is just as strong as the first against the ankle test. Letting the weight fall back on the heels causes the lower back to bend under; like a dog with its tail between its legs. Strong animals extend their tails high. A push-over is a person whose weight has fallen back; who has lost the basic stability of mind and body.

There are other ways to test the stability of the standing posture. Have your partner stand at your side, and press lightly on your chest, using the fingertips of the closest hand, thumb down (Fig. 1-5). Using the closer hand allows your partner to gauge the amount of pressure used. If the opposite hand is used, thumb up, it is too easy to lean the full body weight into the test; or be tempted to shove rather than test gradually. Always compare the incorrect posture with the correct one, using the same degree and direction of strength each time you test. Raising the heels each time you begin the exercise helps the body to form automatic good habits. Like a child, the body needs to be reminded often in order to correct bad habits. Do not abbreviate the tests or fail to practice them once you think you have understood them.

In addition to the ankles and the chest, the wrists can also be used to test mind

Fig. 1-5   Fig. 1-6

and body unity. Let your arms hang naturally at your sides. Ask your partner to try to lift your wrist using only one hand, in the direction of the shoulder (Fig. 1-6). If the posture is correct, then the wrist will not come up, and the shoulder will remain calm and unmoved against the test. This is more difficult than the ankle test. To help coordinate the arms with the rest of the body, first shake the wrists, vigorously enough to move the heels up and down (Fig. 1-7). Two or three seconds is sufficient, as if you were shaking water off of your fingertips. Though your hands appear to come to a stop, feel the vibration continue; getting smaller and smaller, until you lose sight of it. This allows the hands to stop calmly; full of potential energy. Ask your partner to test again, and the difference will be obvious. This is an excellent way to relax or regain composure before an important event.

How to Correct Your Sitting Posture

People who stand with poor posture are not likely to do any better sitting down. Whether sitting cross-legged, or in a chair, most people sit slumped on their tailbone, with their weight back. Some chairs are designed so badly, that it is hard not to sit poorly. It almost seems that the softer and more comfortable, the chair, the weaker the posture. However, it is not necessary to be uncomfortable to sit on the floor or in a chair. A properly unified posture is actually more comfortable,

Fig. 1-7

Fig. 1-8

Fig. 1-9

Fig. 1-10

because it can be easily maintained for long periods. The conventional way of sitting casually is to make oneself comfortable. The problem with this, is that it is a full time job. You cannot slouch for long without having to shift position.

Sitting cross-legged is not much different than standing, except that you have a wider base. If your weight falls back too far, it spreads out across the floor; resulting in a condition similar to flat-footedness. The best way to correct or prevent this, is to raise your tailbone off of the floor, as you did with your heels; lifting yourself by your hands from the floor. Gently set yourself down, as if your legs were very sore, and couldn't bear much weight (Fig. 1-8). Having used your arms to lift yourself off of the ground, there may still be some tension in your shoulders or upper body. Gently loosen your shoulders, and set your hands down comfortably in front of your ankles, completely relaxed (Fig. 1-9). In this posture you almost automatically have mind and body unified. By repeating it as soon as you feel uncomfortable, it is possible to sit this way for hours without fidgeting, while engaged in work or conversation.

In the standing position it is easy to test the ankles. But while sitting cross-legged, it is easier to test the knees. Ask your partner to test with the fingertips, rather than the palm, and to be sure to lift straight up toward the ceiling (Fig. 1-10). This test is far more difficult if your partner leans in with his body weight, using your upper leg as a lever to unbalance you. But even the easier test cannot be passed if you sit on your tailbone (Fig. 1-11). The weight is underside, but properly forward. Therefore lifting the knee feels as hard as if one were trying to lift the whole body.

Having your partner push lightly on your chest will help you to focus on the One Point (Fig. 1-12). However, in the cross-legged position, the One Point is not in the lower abdomen, but below the ankles, even slightly below the floor. Before your partner touches your chest, mentally absorb his Ki into your One Point. Think of the One Point as the calm center of a rapidly swirling whirlpool. If your posture is correct, then your One Point will be able to absorb and neutralize a great deal of external pressure. For comparison, try the same test while picturing your One Point as farther back, inside the abdomen. This brings the weight back and violates the basic principles of Ki, so naturally the body becomes unstable (Fig. 1-13).

It may seem that the best way to resist pressure from behind would be to lean back against it. However, when pushed by your partner on the back with both hands, leaning back only gives him the resistance needed to topple you forward (Fig. 1-14). If you extend Ki strongly and relax completely, then you will neither fall nor slide forward. A lot of pressure may be used, as long as it is applied steadily in a forward direction; don't shove (Fig. 1-15). The test may be easier to pass if you think of your whole body moving forward as a unit, as if sliding on ice. It also helps to stretch the back, as if you were going to stand up. Surprisingly, this makes the whole body firm as a rock; rooted to the ground. However, if you try to stay rooted to the spot, then your body becomes tense, and can be easily tilted or pushed off of its position. The stability afforded by this posture goes beyond the physical test. Sitting in a stable posture gives a person a subtle advantage in a negotiation or confrontation.

When we sit leaning back against a chair or wall, the weight shifts back. If we rely on the back of the chair for support, then we lose the One Point. It is possible to sit comfortably in a chair, in full contact with, but not leaning heavily against the back of the chair. Though this posture looks quite natural, it is very stable against a test from the front (Fig. 1-16). There is no need to stick to any particular posture. It is impossible to maintain mind and body unity or function in daily life by sitting in a rigid, aloof manner.

Fig. 1-11   Fig. 1-12

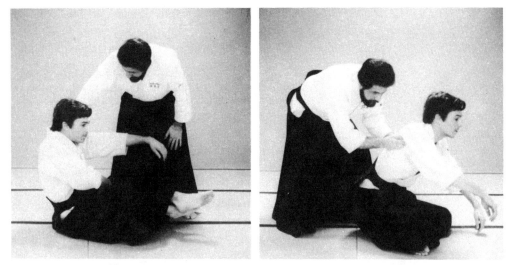

Fig. 1-13   Fig. 1-14

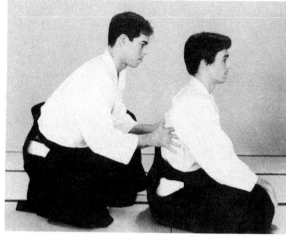

Fig. 1-15

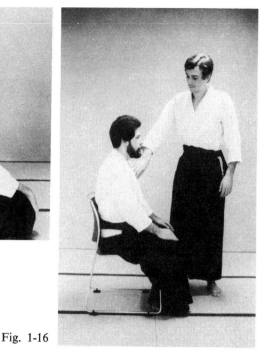

Fig. 1-16

Unified in Any Posture

Fear of heights is something that only seems to go away when we stand on the ground. It is easy to keep balance while leaning on a railing which circles the roof of a tall building. If the railing were not there, we wouldn't dare go near the edge. But the railing only provides a false sense of security. If it were to suddenly tear lose under our weight, we would be likely to fall with it. Leaning on an object brings the weight upperside. But it is possible to lean comfortably on something without losing One Point, if the upper body is relaxed.

Ask your partner to bend forward at the waist, and act as a railing support. Stand to the side and bend forward, keeping the One Point, and letting the full weight of the upper body settle on the underside of your forearms as you lean on your partner's back (Fig. 1-17). Your partner can test your balance by suddenly dropping to the floor at an unexpected moment. Because your arms are completely relaxed, they swing down naturally when he drops to the floor (Fig. 1-18). Because you have your foundation in the One Point, and weight on the balls of the feet, you don't stumble forward or lose your balance. If you hold your arms in the original position after he drops down, it means that your weight was upperside from the beginning (Fig. 1-19). You never really leaned on his back at all.

It is no different leaning back on something, standing or sitting. Stand with one foot in front of the other, leaning the weight of your upper body against your partner's back. The One Point drops down slightly, even moving out in front of your body, but still at the height of your lower abdomen (Fig. 1-20). Your partner

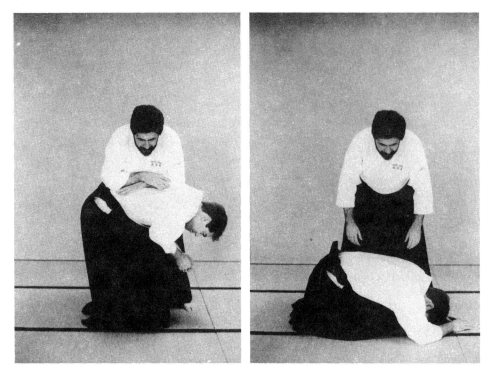

Fig. 1-17

Fig. 1-18

Fig. 1-19

Fig. 1-20

may choose to move away suddenly, any time after he feels the full weight of your body leaning on his back. If you are properly relaxed, and centered at the One Point, then your feet will not move to compensate for the loss of support (Fig. 1-21). Though your full upper body weight was there, it did not cause you to lose your balance. However if you consciously lose any one of the four basic principles, allowing your mind to wander or body to sag back, then you will stumble back when the support is removed (Fig. 1-22). We commonly assume that to really rest or relax, we must give our weight over to the support. Actually the reverse is true. Fatigue is caused by lack of mind and body coordination in our daily movements. Correct relaxation is refreshing. It does not make you lazy; nor does it cut off circulation by putting undue pressure on some part of the body. It is better to get too little than too much sleep; for too little sleep leads to a natural sense of fatigue. Too much sleep makes your spirit weak and sluggish.

We can hardly go a single hour without moving our arms, and assuming various postures other than the ones described here. There is no need to lose mind and body stability just because we move our limbs. If it were lost that easily then Ki training would be of little practical value. Try stretching your arms straight up, as if reaching for the sky. Feel free to stretch them to the limit. Then have your partner test your stability by pushing on your chest (Fig. 1-23). This should be even more stable than the original standing posture. If you raise your arms half-heartedly, short of the full extension, then it will be very difficult to stand up to even a very gentle push (Fig. 1-24). If you move your arms without extending Ki, then tension creeps into the upper body.

Fig. 1-21   Fig. 1-22

Fig. 1-23   Fig. 1-24

The Immovable Mind

In Japanese the word *fudôshin* (不動心) suggests a spirit of unshakable calm and determination. It is courage without recklessness. A person may pretend to have it; but in a crisis the truth will out. The mind cannot be directly perceived, but the body is its weather vane. If the mind is immovable, then the body should be stable.

Because the body is a material object, governed by material laws, it cannot be absolutely immovable. No one can resist the lifting power of an elevator, or the force of an oncoming car. Nor is it necessary to do so when it is possible to move out of the way. Nevertheless *fudôshin* does produce a remarkable degree of rooted stability, in both mental and physical realms.

Stand in the basic unified posture. Calm and focus your mind at the One Point, and ask your partner to attempt to lift your body; placing both of his hands under your armpits, and lifting straight up (Fig. 1-25). If your mind and body are coordinated it should be next to impossible for even a very strong person to lift you. It may seem that your partner is not trying to lift; but when his Ki is absorbed at your One Point, it saps his strength. The contrast is quite clear however, if your partner attempts to lift your body when you deliberately lose mind and body coordination (Fig. 1-26). The contrast may not be as obvious if your partner hasn't the strength to lift you anyway.

Part of the difficulty with the test of the unliftable body, is that it seems to challenge people to use several times as much strength lifting the body in the correct posture. This disqualifies it as a fair test. But if your partner can lift you anyway, he may remain unconvinced. In an effort to overcome your apparent weight, your partner may unconsciously change the angle at which he is lifting. Twisting your body, holding it lower, or pulling you towards him on a backward diagonal can give him added mechanical advantage. If your partner has both superior strength and leverage, he will easily pick your feet off of the ground. To prevent this you can try one of several things. Standing on the balls of your feet as he lifts may neutralize his strength (Fig. 1-27); as will leaning back slightly, letting your wrists lightly touch his forearms near the elbows (Fig. 1-28). He hardly feels this light touch in the struggle, but it acts like a ground wire, returning his strength back to him. But as a rule, any difficulty that you have in being unliftable can be traced to one of the four basic principles.

Why should mind and body unification make the body heavier? Actually the weight does not change at all, unless both people are standing on the same scale. There is no difference in weight between a 30 kilogram suitcase and a 30 kilogram sack of rice; but the grain seems much heavier. It responds differently to incoming stresses, and offers no handle. When the mind is immovable, the body is capable of absorbing tremendous amounts of stress without suffering any damage. This is true strength, as opposed to the apparent or limited strength of large muscles.

Fig. 1-25   Fig. 1-26

Fig. 1-27   Fig. 1-28

The Value of Ki Testing

A thirteenth-century Zen master wrote a story which is still well-known today. In it the patriarch of Zen Buddhism, Bodhidharma, was confronted by his tormented one-armed disciple, asking the master to pacify his troubled mind. Bodhidharma asked his disciple to show him that mind. But the disciple replied that his mind eluded him every time he tried to search for and hold it. Bodhidharma replied, "Then your mind is pacified already."

Bodhidharma's disciple suffered because he could not contain or pacify his mind. When he realized the futility of trying to set limits on his unlimited nature, then he found the immovable mind. Having actually had it all along, he had not understood its true nature.

The four basic principles of mind and body unification explain the nature of *fudôshin*. We can test the validity of the principles for ourselves by testing the stability of the body. However, if the Ki tests are not properly understood and performed, then they degenerate into a mere game. They are not designed for show or for competition. The real value of Ki testing is that it shows us that we cannot learn Ki in isolation from other people. We learn by teaching and testing others, as we learn by being tested. There are hundreds of Ki tests. Only a small sample have been presented here. Furthermore, the difficulty of the tests increases if you test with Ki rather than with physical pressure alone. No two people perform the same test in exactly the same way; so one can never truly master a test by practicing with a single partner. Practice the tests well before you try to demonstrate them to others. Your offer to demonstrate may come across as a challenge, and the added pressure to perform can disturb your One Point. If you do perform the tests for others, do so with the intent to teach them how to do it; not to show off.

The Ki tests are subtle forms of biofeedback. They are useful as a means of comprehending abstract statements about Ki. But only with daily practice do they begin to change the subconscious habits that we have formed. Considerable practice and personal feedback from a qualified instructor is the fastest and most reliable way of learning to coordinate mind and body in daily life.

The greatest obstacle to progress in Ki development is thinking that you already know. A mind open to feedback is strong in Ki already. By nature Ki is elusive; capable of being directed but not contained by the mind. There is no hope of realizing it without regular, lifelong practice; both in Ki exercise and in daily movements. Keeping the One Point under stress will open your eyes to the hidden opportunities in the situation. Managing to truly relax in the face of danger or risk will strengthen your immovable mind. With practice your confidence will grow. But it takes time to let the subconscious mind restructure its orientation to problems. If you help others grow by teaching them what you have learned, then you will benefit the more. If you do not share your knowledge then you will lose it; as Ki is a universal energy, which cannot be contained by the mind.

2. KI Development

The Mind Moves the Body

The goal of Ki training is mind and body coordination, in any activity, including sleep. It is relatively easy to unify mind and body while standing or sitting, consciously practicing one of the four basic principles. But if your partner tests you a second time, a moment or two after you have successfully passed a Ki test, you may find that you have already lost it in that brief moment. If you are tested at an unexpected moment, the lack of stability is even more obvious. And it is more difficult still to maintain mind and body coordination in movement. Yet as long as we live, we can not avoid movement. If Ki training is to be of any practical value, it must be possible to maintain the four principles in any activity; at work, at rest, and at play.

There are dozens of exercises for training Ki in movement. All of them are based on the same fundamental premise: that the mind leads the body. Without motivation we would be helpless to do anything. Some motivations are physical, like the need to satisfy hunger. Others involve psychological or emotional rewards. But all motivations are perceived and acted on by the mind. Motivation can be self-directed; or it can originate in the pressures and urgings of other people. Typically, motivation is stimulated by random, external influences. The resulting passive behavior ultimately leads to a feeling of powerlessness. When motivation is self-directed, it results in greater control and a sense of mastery.

There are many approaches to self-control; including hypnosis, time management, and psychological techniques. But without understanding the true nature of mind and body unity, it is impossible to transcend technique. Graceful performance of any skill depends on self-mastery; in other words, mastery of the mind. Though governed by different principles, the mind and body are closely connected, like horse and cart. The expression, "putting the cart before the horse" is used when a person tries to act unreasonably. Yet this is what we usually do when we try to learn a new skill. In the beginning we have only a vague mental image of what we are trying to do. This naturally produces an imperfect result; we miss the target, we stumble over our words. In our eagerness to get it right, we send the body into action without a clear idea of what we are doing. Putting the cart before the horse only produces frustration. This disturbs the mind and stresses the body. The immediate result is poor performance. The long-term result is fatigue and illness.

The mind leads the body, but each according to its principles. The mind works most effectively when it is calmly focused at the One Point. The body performs at its best when all stress is released from it. When the horse leads the cart, both function at their best. Most of the difficulty in coordinating mind and body in daily life comes from misunderstanding this simple process. When properly unified, you can direct your full power to any task. Then calm and action become one. A rapidly spinning top seems poised in perfect stillness; yet it whirls away at the slightest touch.

How to Walk with Ki

Perhaps you have experienced walking along a familiar path in the dark, only to suddenly bump into an unexpected object in your path. If the object is big enough, the force of the collision is enough to knock you flat on your back. Stubbing one's toe can also be very painful. Ordinarily, by effort alone we could never generate that much power in movement. But when the mind moves freely ahead, the body follows with surprising power. By directing our mind purposefully toward an objective, we can learn to use this power positively.

Ask your partner to stand in a stable position somewhat in front of you, but just out of your walking path. Walk forward at normal speed, with a positive sense of expectation, as if you were going to meet a good friend. Just before you walk by your partner, have him reach up and across to try to stop you (Fig. 2-1). He should use the hand farthest away from you for greatest leverage. He should grab your opposite shoulder rather than choke your neck. If you extend Ki strongly before you begin to walk, then his resistance will hardly be felt. He will be swept along in your path (Fig. 2-2). If you forget your original objective, that of going to meet someone, then your mind will focus on trying to overcome your partner's

Fig. 2-1   Fig. 2-2

resistance. This causes your body to tense up; to lose Ki extension and power, and you can easily be stopped (Fig. 2-3). It is not necessary to move quickly or to struggle. Just keep one or more of the basic principles clearly in mind before you begin to walk. If you walk with mixed feelings about where you are going, you can be stopped without any effort. If you calm your mind at the One Point before you set yourself to any task, your performance and self-control will improve.

If you walk in this way, your partner should be equally unable to restrain you, even if he clasps one of your ankles with both hands. Allow him to sit close enough to your leg to get a firm grip (Fig. 2-4). If your weight is back on your heels then you will be unable to walk freely; as if you were dragging a ball and chain. However, if you stand in the natural posture, and first find the One Point before taking a step, then you should be able to stroll forward slowly as if nothing were holding you back. Your partner will be dragged forward off-balance, and may have to release your leg to keep from being dragged across the floor (Fig. 2-5).

The formal curriculum of the Ki Society International includes dozens of exercises for Ki development. A few will be explained here in some detail. Ki development exercises make use of rhythm and repetition. The pace is measured by counting aloud. As the voice is part of the body, it too is led by the mind; just as a singer hears a note the moment before singing it. The count need not be loud, however it should get one's attention. A full-bodied abdominal voice is best achieved when there is no tension in the throat or abdominal muscles. Good voice projection and rhythm begin in the mind, with powerful Ki extension. The voice can be forced to make a loud sound; but this results in stiff shoulders and a mecha-

Fig. 2-3

Fig. 2-4

nical rhythm. The mind leads the count; the count leads the body. Each follows the other closely, like a row of dominoes. Because they appear to be almost simultaneous, it takes close attention to keep the body's movement from getting ahead of the count. If this sequence is wrong, it gradually upsets the rhythm of the entire exercise.

Fig. 2-5

Fig. 2-6

Fig. 2-7

Fig. 2-8

Fig. 2-9

Rolling Back and Forth (*Kôhô-Tentô-Undô*) —————————

It is relatively easy to sit cross-legged with mind and body unified beginning in a static position. It is another thing altogether to maintain it after a dynamic motion like rocking back and forth.

Begin in the unified posture, maintaining the One Point, and extending Ki strongly forward (Fig. 2-6). Your partner stands at your side and counts, "One!" Feeling a wave of Ki sweep over your body from a great distance in front of you, roll back on your spine, along its natural curve. At the same time push off of the floor with your ankles (Fig. 2-7). Follow the wave of Ki with your eyes, getting a clear view of the ceiling as you roll back (Fig. 2-8). Keep your chin tucked slightly forward so that your head barely touches the floor, if at all (Fig. 2-9). Just before you naturally rock back, your partner counts "Two!" Feel a fresh wave of new Ki coming from well behind you; sweeping you forward to your original seated position (Fig. 2-10). Throughout the exercise, maintain the same angle and distance between the ankles and shoulders. The feet should describe a large arc in the air on the way back, and return along the same line. Your forward momentum and Ki extension will allow you to stop in this position with perfect composure; needing no adjustment, and without your weight or head dropping back at all.

Though the body motion stops, Ki extension continues on indefinitely, like a jet disappearing into the distance. Then you will be completely relaxed, in a unified posture as before. After you come forward, ask your partner to push on your shoulders from the front, using both hands, thumbs to the outside (Fig. 2-11). As in the static exercise, you should be as stable as a tree. It is important however, that your partner test with the strength of the arms and fingertips. Shoving suddenly, or leaning in with full body weight is not an acceptable test. The knees and shoulders may move slightly in response to the test; which means that the mind is still not calm. If you absorb your partner's Ki at your One Point, then you will not move. Your partner will feel as though he were attempting something beyond his strength.

Fig. 2-10

Fig. 2-11

It is very easy to lose mind and body unification in movement. Moving the body before fully extending Ki or finding the One Point, causes the body to move in an uncoordinated, disjointed fashion. If the upper body moves slightly before the lower body, then the body moves in two pieces. If the head rocks back slightly at the end of the motion, this is a clear sign of tension, or weak Ki extension. These disturbances may be very subtle and hard to observe, but they are easy to test. If your partner pauses a moment before pushing on your shoulders (Fig. 2-12), it will clearly magnify any distortions in your movement, causing you to lean forward or rock back. Even a rather mild test will overcome a mind that is not calm and focused. If the knees rise up, and the chin juts forward, then the weight of the entire body falls back onto the tailbone, and you will have no ground to sit on (Fig. 2-13).

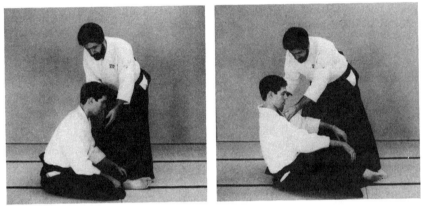

Fig. 2-12   Fig. 2-13

Calm and Focus the Mind at the One Point in the Lower Abdomen

Static postures are inherently stable, making it relatively easy to keep the One Point. Any body movement which does not originate from the One Point is inherently unstable. Yet move we must. To further clarify the meaning of the four basic principles of mind and body unification, Master Tôhei developed additional principles to give perspective on each one.

1. Find the Point in the Lower Abdomen which You Cannot Feel: Old Zen and martial arts texts advise putting strength into the abdomen. In English, a person with courage is said to have guts. To gird oneself is to tighten the belt for action. All of these expressions are misleading. They mistake a mental principle or attitude, keeping One Point, for a place to put physical strength. In fact, assuming that your posture is correct, the One Point is the place in the lower abdomen where you cannot flex a muscle or get any visceral feeling. This calm focal point is the intersection of mind and body.

2. Don't Put Any Weight on the Legs or Feet: Strictly speaking, the weight of the body does fall on the feet, or whatever part is in contact with the ground. But if you allow this feeling to become conscious, you lose the sense of buoyancy which comes from true relaxation. In a correct posture, the weight of the upper body falls on the One Point. Gravity keeps the body's weight underside; but the centrifugal force of the earth's rotation gives it a slight lift or buoyancy. When pressed hard against the ground, most objects will rebound as soon as the pressure is released. Gravity is the stronger of the two forces, but if we let it dominate our awareness, then our weight tends to sag. When the mind is bright and clear then the body is naturally buoyant. Dark moods cause us to lose the One Point, producing fatigue and frustration. It is only possible to put tension into the lower abdomen if the body is bent under a heavy mind. It doesn't require any muscular effort to take the weight off of your feet.

3. Maintain a Posture in which Your Breathing is Calm and Subtle: Rough or labored breathing occurs when the One Point is lost. Illness produces it; as does losing one's temper, or moving in an inefficient manner. Even after running or doing heavy exercise, a calm One Point will bring breathing back to normal after only a moment or so. The breathing of a mindful person is so calm that the transition between breaths is almost imperceptible to other people. It is easy to breathe like this when you maintain the One Point.

4. Maintain an Attitude in Which Nothing Disturbs Your Composure: The One Point is like a great ocean, having the power to accept all things without changing itself. When others around you panic, you can keep things from getting out of control by controlling yourself, keeping One Point. Your mental composure will be reflected by a relaxed and centered posture. This is not an attitude of unconcern or indifference. Rather it is a posture which in a crisis can only be maintained by a mature and aware individual.

5. Keep Calm so that You Can Release Your Full Power at any Time: Some people spend all of their energy in activity; others fail to accumulate enough to get started. The One Point can store tremendous reserve energy, which we can use any time without fear of depletion. With the One Point we can see clearly and act without wasted effort. It gives us the necessary reserves of physical strength to accomplish whatever we need to do. This is the source of the strength that people sometimes find in an emergency, when they accomplish tasks beyond their ordinary physical strength. But we need not wait for a crisis. We can coordinate mind and body in any situation.

The Boat-Rowing Exercise (*Funa-Kogi-Undô*) —————

Though you may understand the theory of how to operate a vehicle, until you can actually drive a car by yourself, you cannot truthfully say that you know how to drive. Similarly, you cannot really say you know the One Point, until you can actually demonstrate and use it. Verbal explanations merely point the way. The Boat-Rowing Exercise is used to help find the One Point in motion. It resembles the rowing motion not of a Western style rowboat with two oars; but of a traditional Japanese craft, with a single oar in the stern of the boat, serving as both rudder and paddle.

All movements in this exercise should originate from the One Point. Counting aloud to lead into the body movement should help maintain the correct rhythm. The arm and hip motions are easy to perform, but difficult to describe. For the sake of clarity, they will be broken down into a series of steps.

Begin in the basic standing posture, feet spread apart at shoulder width, at about a 45-degree angle. Extend Ki strongly, and step forward with one foot. The feet should be between one and two foot lengths apart. A line from each foot would intersect at right angles. At the same time, let the thumb and forefinger of each hand come forward with the hips, touching the body at the level of the One Point. The elbows are slightly bent, but the arms are relaxed. Extend Ki strongly with the mind, but don't puff out the chest or distort the original position of the shoulders (Fig. 2-14). Your partner can test you by pushing on your chest; or from the rear on the lower back. The test should be done perpendicularly to the body; not on a diagonal. The ankles can also be tested by lifting toward the One Point. The exercise really begins from this posture, so it is important that it be stable. Throughout the movement, it is important that the eyes face forward to the horizon, and not look down at the ground.

The forward rowing motion begins with the count of "One!" Return to the original position follows the count of "Two!" Counting can be done by either the person performing the exercise, or the person doing the testing. As in the rolling exercise, the forward moving Ki continues on indefinitely. On the second count, completely new Ki flows in from the horizon, like the current of a strong river. The important thing is to make the movements with a big feeling. For now, leave the wrists on the hips and just practice moving the One Point back and forth in the proper rhythm, without tensing the upper body. The One Point should move parallel to the ground, as if on a rail. Though the movement feels large, it covers only a small distance. The forward knee should not extend beyond the forward toe (Fig. 2-15). According to the second principle of keeping One Point, no weight should be put on the legs or feet. The movement should be small and level enough that no tension is felt above the knees in the thighs. Stability before, during, or after movement can be tested in the same way as before.

Once the hip motion is both comfortable and correct, you can add the arm movement. The movement of the hands feels much bigger than that of the One Point. The chest should feel expansive; but not swell and contract with each mo-

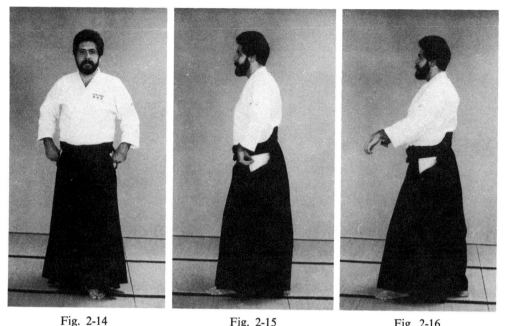

Fig. 2-14   Fig. 2-15   Fig. 2-16

tion. The hands move straight forward from the hips after the One Point reaches its forward position; like an arrow shot from a bow. They come to a stop with the wrists bent at about 45 degrees, fingertips curled under. When they come to a stop they cause a very mild and pleasant vibration in the neck and shoulders. The arms feel stretched, but the elbows remain slightly bent; so that if you dropped the arms to your sides from that position, they would feel natural and comfortable without making any adjustments (Fig. 2-16).

Your partner may test you by pushing with both hands on both of your wrists, in the direction of the shoulders (Fig. 2-17). There should be no independent movement in the shoulder joint; which remains calm and undisturbed throughout the entire exercise. If you maintain the One Point, it will absorb your partner's Ki, and he will feel as though he were trying to move a large stone. If there is any tension in the arms they will collapse or move under the test.

It is possible to pass this test by leaning one's body weight forward against the partner's pressure, like a tug of war in reverse. But this is only strong from one direction. If your partner suddenly changes the direction by pulling back on your wrists, it will clearly reveal whether you are using body weight or One Point. When performed properly; a unified posture is strong from any direction.

The back stroke is performed by leaving the hands in place, and moving the hips back on the count of "Two!" The hands may come up slightly in so doing, to waist level. When the hips reach the rear position, the arms follow. Though the arms are completely relaxed, they have enough power to pull your partner totally off balance. In the forward position, ask your partner to grab both of your wrists with his hands. Without putting any tension in the shoulders, keeping the upper body vertical, lead back with the hips to take up the slack in the arms (Fig. 2-18),

Fig. 2-17   Fig. 2-18

Fig. 2-19

and bring your wrists back to your hips, pulling your opponent off-balance (Fig. 2-19).

When done without stopping, as a solitary exercise, the sequence for the movement is: hips forward, hands forward, hips back, hands back. This is done rhythmically, but without stopping for a test; taking about one second for each stroke, leaving a slight pause in between to feel the Ki movement. After at least eight strokes on one side, the feet are reversed and the same thing is repeated on the other side. Like a golf swing, the arm and hip motion in the Boat-Rowing Exercise are simple in form, but difficult to master. It bears much repetition, each time going back to fundamental principles. The purpose of this exercise and others is to develop Ki; not to build muscles, lose weight, or wear oneself out. Ki exercises cultivate inner strength. From this comes an enduring strength based on self-control and efficient use of the body.

Completely Release All Stress from the Body ——————————

As with the One Point, there are five principles for better understanding what is meant by complete relaxation. It is the body, not the mind which relaxes completely.

1. Release All Stress in the Body, So That Each Part Settles in Its Natural Position: Excess tension accumulates unconsciously, particularly in the shoulders. Driving a car for many hours, or working without a break; we eventually become aware of how tense we have become. A person who makes a habit of storing tension in this way can become so stiff that even massage or rest doesn't help. Eventually he may not even know where to put his neck and shoulders. Total relaxation by muscular flaccidity is no antidote to this condition. A limp body can only come from a limp mind. This condition is too dull and sluggish to refresh the body. It puts undue pressure on the internal organs and restricts blood circulation; actually accelerating the aging process. True relaxation is only possible when each part of the body settles in its natural position, not when the muscles are flaccid. There is no genuine relaxation without an alert mind.

2. Relax Positively, without Collapsing or Losing Power: Exertion naturally causes fatigue. The body operates within its physical limitations. The mind is free of such restraints. It need never give in to the fatigue of the body unless it gives up its leading role. A positive attitude allows the body to rest and recuperate continually, without losing any of its strength or resiliency. Relaxation without Ki is powerless and impotent.

3. Maintain a Posture which Projects a Sense of Expansion: Many professional actors or athletes are of average height, but the good ones always look big on the stage or the playing field. Skilled professionals are very relaxed at what they do, even under pressure. Calmness in the face of pressure makes a person seem bigger than life. It is the very opposite of the person who collapses into a chair in an effort to unwind. A diminutive appearance has more to do with tension than with actual physical size.

4. Be Strong Enough to be Relaxed: That relaxation is better, is common sense; that relaxation is stronger, takes special insight to appreciate. Yet it is self-evident in the Ki tests; which show that a relaxed body is stable, resilient, and capable of generating surprising energy. A body which is tensed to resist is unsteady, brittle, and restricted in its movements. Raw muscular strength can lift heavy objects; but it is no guarantee of health or happiness.

5. Maintain an Attitude of Non-Dissension: It takes two to make an argument. Insecure people are always jockeying for position or competing for attention. Lacking a center of strength in the One Point, they find it difficult to relax or accept things as they are. When you know that relaxation and Ki will protect you, it is easy to relax and set worries aside. However, though holding your tongue may prevent an argument; even if you say nothing, when you clash with other people in your mind it builds resistance. This registers as tension in your body. Compliance and compromise are no easy answer; they may only mask timidity. Timid people shrink from conflict. A truly courageous person can relax in the face of it.

The Arm-Swinging Exercise (*Ude-Mawashi-Undô*)

The shoulders become stiff when they are moved off-center of the shoulder joint. This exercise involves swinging the arms with the shoulder joint as the center of the circle. The mechanics of the Arm-Swinging Exercise are deceptively simple. But when performed properly, it releases and prevents shoulder stiffness. Though it feels quite relaxed, it generates enough force to throw a person to the ground.

Begin in the unified standing posture. Shake the wrists and fingertips as described in Fig. 1-7, to completely release all stress from the body. As a conductor raises the baton to start a performance, raise one hand straight up. Fingers relaxed, raise the arm as high as it goes without straightening the elbow (Fig. 2-20). Closely following the count of "One!", allow the hand to drop down at the speed of a light towel (Fig. 2-21). Near the waist, let the momentum of the swing carry the arm back and up to its original top position, making one revolution (Fig. 2-22). The count of "Two!" begins the hand's second revolution around the shoulder joint.

Fig. 2-20   Fig. 2-21   Fig. 2-22

Each swing takes between one and two seconds. The hand should move like a ball on the end of a string; smoothly, without jerking the arm or stopping. After four swings on one side, make four swings with the other arm; alternating sides until you have performed four sets of four on each side.

There is a tendency to bring the arm down too far; in an effort to gain a sense of doing a vigorous exercise. But this actually produces the reverse effect: moving the shoulder joint up and down, so that the hand and shoulder really revolve around a center point between them. The hand should revolve around the shoulder joint, which itself remains calm and undisturbed by the motion. Moving the arm down too far causes it to jerk at the lowest part of the swing; disturbing mind and body coordination, because no part of the body is allowed to settle at its natural position. The correct way of swinging the arm may feel too high at first. But it is correct if the shoulder joint stays at the center. The hand describes an oval shape; somewhat to the side, but within the field of peripheral vision. Both downswing and upswing are done at an even speed, but there is a slight hesitation at the top of the swing to allow for the leading motion of Ki with the count.

Because of long years of habitually using the arm and shoulder incorrectly, it may feel strange to swing the arm in this way. If we are accustomed to moving and exercising only the body, without consciously extending Ki, then it may feel as though you were not doing any exercise at all. There is no benefit in repeating the arm swing unless it is done correctly. Once the rhythm and form are mastered, alternating sets of ten swings per side, you may practice between one to five hundred swings; and its benefit as a physical exercise will become apparent. The hardest habit to overcome is the tendency to speed up on the downstroke, in an

Fig. 2-23   Fig. 2-24   Fig. 2-25

effort to get a feeling of physical exertion or power. However the power of the arm swing derives from Ki, not the speed or strength of the arm. To better visualize the rhythm of the swing, you can use the index finger of the other hand to point out the leading motion of Ki. Move the index finger in a slightly smaller radius than the hand doing the exercise, and drop it at a slightly faster rate (Figs. 2-23, 24, and 25). Ki is not restricted by physical time or distance, so it can freely move ahead of the arm. However, mind and body are connected, like horse and cart. The Ki should not move ghost-like, totally independent of the body; it should lead and precede the arm's falling motion.

The Arm-Swinging Exercise begins in the upper position, and ends with the arm hanging at rest at your side. When the arm swings past the waist, there is almost no sensation of the hand or wrist, because it does not jerk the arm. This is also true at the end of the exercise, when the arm comes to rest. At first, it may even feel as though the elbows were bent, and the arms shorter than they should be. The arms should hang freely from the center of the shoulder joint; not dangle from the top or bottom of it. When the posture is unified, it is easy to find the center of the shoulder joint, and let the arms relax completely. At the end of the exercise, the wrists should be tested as in Fig. 1-6. Or they may be pulled down strongly toward the floor. If the arm is in the proper position, the wrist can easily support the dangling weight of a full grown person (Fig. 2-26). But if there is any tension in the arm or shoulder, then even a fraction of that weight will pull you off balance. This test is a good way to learn how to carry a heavy suitcase without fatigue.

Fig. 2-26   Fig. 2-27

The power of a fully relaxed arm becomes evident when you try to offer an obstacle to its motion. Ask your partner to extend his arm at shoulder height, making a fist and bracing his body in a position to resist the downward motion of your arm. First test the strength of his resistance by pushing down on his elbow with your hand, using physical force. If he can easily resist this force, then he will believe that he can easily stop the motion of your arm on the downswing. Stand behind your partner, and extend the same side arm as he has extended. Facing the same direction, perform the first three swings without touching his arm. If your Ki extension is strong, he will feel the power and size of your arm movement before you touch his arm, even if the arm swing is only visible from the corner of his eye. Without changing anything about your motion, simply turn 90 degrees and perform the fourth swing coming down on his elbow with your forearm. By the time your arm touches his elbow, your Ki should have already penetrated it (Fig. 2-27). Rather than speeding up to overcome the resistance of the arm, feel as though you are slowing down. This will maintain the rhythm. Even if he resists strongly, you should be able to move his arm aside as if it was not even there; possibly even unbalancing or throwing him to the ground (Fig. 2-28). But any trace of tension, any loss of mind and body unity on your part will cause your arm to stop and bounce back off of his elbow. The only thing that moves in this case is your shoulder joint (Fig. 2-29). When the shoulder is off-center, the arm is powerless to overcome an obstacle. If the strain is too great, as in a contact sport, it may even dislocate the shoulder.

Fig. 2-28   Fig. 2-29

Let the Weight of Every Part of the Body Settle Naturally at its Lowest Point ——————————————————————————————————

As with relaxation, the principles for keeping weight underside deal more with the body than the mind. The hardest thing about keeping weight underside is simply allowing it to happen. Gravity keeps the weight down naturally. If we push an object down with any additional force, we meet resistance from centrifugal force; actually bringing the weight upperside. In a body at rest, the weight naturally falls on the lowest side; the side closest to the center of the earth. Movement does not change the principle of weight underside, but it may change the place on which the weight falls. When the body bends forward, when the limbs move, or when a person spins around, centrifugal force throws the weight to the outer edges, away from the center line. If the body spins fast enough, it becomes momentarily weightless. A figure skater seems to hover above the ice while skating, but comes back down when standing at rest. When we interfere with the small but significant amount of centifugal force operating on our body in motion then the body becomes tense, in an effort to maintain balance. We do not usually become aware of this process until we attempt a difficult movement. Tension fights the motion, destroying its grace and power. The result is awkwardness, dizziness, or loss of balance.

1. Maintain the Most Comfortable Posture: The most natural posture should be the most comfortable one. Still the most common posture that we assume for the sake of comfort is slouched and leaning against a support. Ironically, the more comfortable the posture, the more quickly it is abandoned for another, similarly slumped position. The luxury of poor posture is illusory. The only relief it provides is temporary; easing the strain on one set of muscles, only to apply it to another. Poor posture ultimately leads to health problems. Any posture in which mind and body are unified is possible to maintain for a long period of time, with minimal adjustments, if any. The person who can maintain good posture in the midst of vigorous movement can keep weight underside, moving with maximum grace and control.

2. Let Your Weight Fall Naturally so that It does not Feel Heavy: The moment that you are conscious of the weight of your body at any point, then it is probably sagging, rather than falling naturally. An ailing liver or stomach makes its presence felt. There is no joy in a heavy head or heart. Favoring an injury by limping, we become aware of the weight of both legs. When we feel depressed, we drag our feet. There are hardly any positive expressions which suggest the body feeling heavy. Keeping the weight underside is not the same as feeling heavy. Rather, it is a state of buoyancy; responsive to both gravity and centrifugal force.

3. Fully Extend Your Ki: You cannot keep weight underside without extending Ki. They are both aspects of the same thing. But in a static position the weight falls underside; in a dynamic movement the weight falls to the outside as well. This is as true for the smallest gesture as for the most vigorous motion, only a matter of degree. In any case, Ki should be fully extended before the motion begins. The physical power generated by the movement depends primarily on this Ki extension. Nothing need be done with the body to put the weight underside, other than maintain correct posture and extend Ki.

4. Be Quick and Flexible in Response to All Circumstances: If the weight is underside, settled but not heavy, then the body is fully ready for action. Japanese *samurai* were once trained to leave their sandals side by side near the door, facing outward in the event of an emergency. A person who left his shoes in a state of disarray, or couldn't find them, was considered to be dangerously unsettled, and unprepared for even the simple duties of daily life. Completing small actions that you begin is an excellent way to keep weight underside. It requires that you direct your Ki to whatever you do, and allows centrifugal force to operate freely in your body.

5. See and Hear Everything around You Clearly: When the breezes stop blowing across the surface of a lake, the waves and ripples settle down and the surface reflects everything clearly. The only thing you can do to make water in a basin settle down is to leave it alone. Even very rough waters are always in the process of settling down, because that is the nature of water. The weight of our body will do the same if we let it. Whether at rest or in motion, its natural tendency is to settle down. In a calm state, the senses become very sharp; quick to pick up on subtle changes in our environment.

Turning and Spinning Exercise (*Tenkan-Undô*)

Begin with the same foot position as in the Boat-Rowing Exercise. Raise the wrist on the same side as the forward foot. The arm moves in a short upward arc, stopping when the wrist reaches about navel height (Fig. 2-30). The ankles, wrist, chest, and back can be tested for stability.

After a strong forward extension of Ki, let the back hand which is hanging at your side come forward. Stepping through at the same time with the back foot, bring the hips up to the position of the forward hand (Fig. 2-31). Continuing to extend your Ki in a forward direction, pivot on the ball of the stepping foot, turning 180 degrees to face the rear. Draw the other foot back after you turn, to maintain the proper distance between the feet. The end result is a mirror image of how you started, with the other hand and foot forward. The hand is still extended, but now the palm is face up, thumb to the outside (Fig. 2-32).

This same motion is repeated, to a count, in four sets of four turns. The exercise begins with Ki extension leading into a forward motion, followed by a quick turn, and ending in a calm and balanced pause. This pause is not really a full stop.

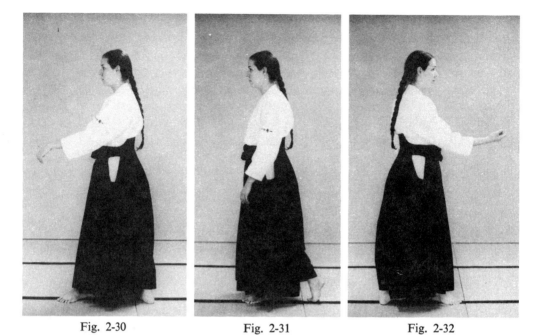

Fig. 2-30   Fig. 2-31   Fig. 2-32

It is like a bird suddenly swooping down from above and alighting on a branch. If the mind and body are unified throughout the turn then it is easy to stop calmly. But if the weight is thrown upperside, then tension throws the body off balance. If a deep step is taken, it is necessary to compensate for the extra distance by lightly sliding the forward foot back into position after you turn.

The secret to the entire turn is extending Ki strongly before you move. But Ki cannot be perceived directly by the senses, so it may be necessary to find some indirect way of measuring it. Hold a light hand towel in the hand that is to be extended. Release it from the fingertips as you bring the hand forward for the first time. If Ki moves before the hand, then the towel will hit the ground at least a meter in front of the hand, even though you do not attempt to throw it (Figs. 2-33, 34, and 35). If you move the hand before extending Ki, then the towel will drop to the ground more or less directly below the hand, even if you try to extend Ki on the way up (Fig. 2-36).

Maintaining the proper distance between the feet at the end of the exercise is also quite difficult. If you do the turn within a small radius, without much forward motion, the forward foot merely steps and pivots, and the back foot simply swings around to the rear. However, if you take a large forward step and cover more distance, then the back foot covers a proportionately larger distance, and the forward foot must slide back as you end the turn, in order to compensate for the extra distance (Fig. 2-37). This sliding motion should be made lightly, with the ball of the foot. The posture should be straight and tall, with an expansive feeling. Dragging the foot along the heel brings the weight upperside. Unless you fully extend your Ki, move quickly and flexibly, then you can be easily unbalanced by a Ki test at the moment that you stop.

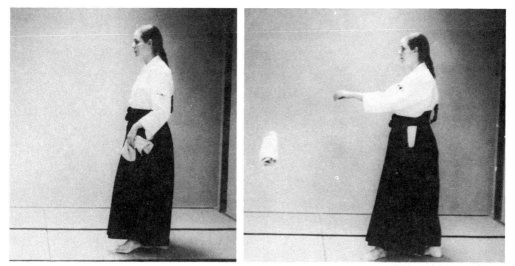

Fig. 2-33   Fig. 2-34

Fig. 2-35   Fig. 2-36

It is easy to perform the turning exercise when your wrist and arm meet no resistance. Your partner can apply some resistance by grabbing your wrist tightly with one hand. If your left arm is extended, ask your partner to use his right hand, palm down, applying pressure with the base of the index finger and gripping your wrist with the little finger, as if holding a tennis racquet. It then becomes very difficult to turn without raising your shoulder, or feeling pain in the wrist. If you use your free hand to gently pull the fingertips of the held hand (Fig. 2-38), then you can turn or pull your partner forward without feeling any resistance (Fig. 2-39). This simple action directs the mind to move ahead of the fingertips, helping you to extend Ki and keep the weight underside. Because your partner's resistance is hardly even felt, you move in the most comfortable posture.

Fig. 2-37   Fig. 2-38

Fig. 2-39   Fig. 2-40

If you make multiple turns before coming to a stop, then the turning exercise becomes a spinning exercise. The centrifugal force is much greater when you spin, tending to lift your arms to the outside as you turn. Keeping the arms in closer to the hips as you turn will make it easier to keep balance. Instead of stopping to face the rear, simply continue moving the One Point forward as you spin, pivoting on one foot after the other. After making two, three, or even more turns, come out of the spin by facing what was the rear direction. Let the hand come out palm up as before. Be sure that the final posture is correctly upright (Fig. 2-40). Because the centrifugal force is greater, the turn tends to pull the weight to the outside. If your body becomes tense from resisting this movement, then you become confused about where to put the feet while you spin. The result is a loss of mind and body unity, and a loss of balance.

It is more difficult to spin than to turn. It is easier to maintain mind and body unity in a static posture than in the midst of vigorous activity. Yet unless we can do both, then we will be unprepared to face either the routine tasks or the crises of life.

Extend Ki

Extending Ki is a principle of the mind, but it does not mean to extend the mind, Ki and the mind are not the same thing. Ki is a universal energy; the mind is our ability to open or close ourselves off to that energy. Nor can we extend Ki merely by stretching the body. Extending the arms and fingers may create the appearance of extending Ki, but it may also violate the principle of totally relaxing the body. Moving the body before the mind, we may wind up extending only the arm, without Ki. There is a limit to how far you can stretch or extend your body, but Ki can be extended without limit, to the ends of the universe.

1. Maintain a Posture in which You are Unconscious of Your Body: A person who is burdened with mental or physical problems is all too conscious of his body. This is a sign that Ki extension is weak. The best way to begin to solve those problems, whatever their nature, is to extend strong Ki. A hose which emits a strong jet of water, not only flushes itself clean, but effectively prevents any foreign object from entering the nozzle.

2. Let Centrifugal Force have Full Play: As shown in Fig. 2-34, strong Ki extension generates strong centrifugal force. The trajectory of the towel shows the extension of the Ki line made by the arm's movement. Ki extension is under our direct conscious control, centrifugal force is not. Even the smallest motion has centrifugal force. Yet we are not even conscious of the very powerful centrifugal forces operating on us all of the time, such as that produced by the earth in its rotation or revolution about the sun.

3. Show Kindness in Your Face, Eyes, and Voice. A person with truly strong Ki does not use it to take advantage of others. That strength and composure can be used to help others whenever possible. People are naturally drawn to someone who has a strong spirit and a composed manner. The eyes and voice are sensitive indicators of both a person's mental and physical condition. They are good ways to gauge Ki extension. Likewise, if you would extend Ki more effectively, you can do so through the eyes and the voice.

4. Show Composure in Your Posture: Ki should not be mistaken for excitement, or wild energetic behavior. In many sports and martial arts, a relaxed body is capable of generating a great deal more power than one which is clenched and tight. Because you are strong and free of anxiety, you can afford to be composed.

5. Enjoy what You do without Anxiety over Results: Extending Ki frees the spirit. The spirit is only free when it is self-directed; not the puppet of circumstances and other people. This is not a license for uninhibited behavior. The body can remain calm because it has no need to prove itself. If the mind can clearly direct itself to the task at hand, it can do what needs to be done and have faith in a positive outcome. Walking forward with a sense of positive expectation has the power to brush obstacles aside.

Forward Hand Swing (*Ikkyô-Undô*) ———————

Stand in the unified posture. Move one foot forward, but in this case, the thumbs are let hang naturally. The fingers are curled in a very loose fist (Fig. 2-41). On the count of "One!", with strong Ki extension, move the hips and arms forward together with the One Point. Without letting the knee go beyond the toes of the forward foot, allow the hands to continue forward in an upward arc, until the fingertips are pointing up, at about eye level (Fig. 2-42). On the count of "Two!", bring the hands straight down on the same arc, without moving the hips (Fig. 2-43). When they reach the hips, bring them back together with the One Point to the original position. The motion is performed in one smooth sequence. It follows the order of: hips forward, hands up, hands down, hips back.

The stability of the body may be tested by pushing on the hands after the count

Fig. 2-41   Fig. 2-42   Fig. 2-43

Fig. 2-44   Fig. 2-45

of one (Fig. 2-44), or on the back (Fig. 2-45). A hand towel may be used as in Fig. 2-34, to see whether or not Ki is being strongly extended. Extending Ki is easily confused with extending the arms. Too much arm extension may be strong against a test from the front, but is very weak against a test from the back. It takes practice to realize that Ki extends most naturally when the body is completely relaxed. Extending Ki may cause the eyes and chest to expand; but the reverse is not true, because the mind leads the body.

A variation on the forward hand swing is done in four counts; "One-Two" (up-down) to the front, and "Three-Four" (up-down) to the rear. In this case the hips are not drawn back on the second count, but left in the forward position for the turn. Pivot on the ball of the forward foot, which becomes the back foot after you turn 180 degrees to the rear. Allow the back foot to float and barely touch the ground as you turn. The whole set of four counts is repeated four times. Have your partner test you on the lower back as you turn and begin to move forward. This is potentially the most unstable moment, so it is a good test of mind and body coordination in movement. The test should be performed in a straight forward direction. However, if you try to move out of rhythm or cut corners in your turn, then even a straight test will be received on a diagonal, and cause you to lose your balance.

If our mind wanders in performing any task, then unconsciously our Ki extension grows weaker. Swinging the hands back and forth, to the front and to the back, requires you to consciously direct your mind one hundred percent in whatever direction you turn. Otherwise your body becomes very unstable. Because the arc described by the hands is rather small, it is easy for the Ki movement to grow

Fig. 2-46   Fig. 2-47

smaller with each swing; when in fact the opposite should happen. The strength of the Ki extension can be tested by having your partner resist the movement of your wrists up from the hips at count one (Fig. 2-46). If the Ki extension is weak, then the wrist can easily be stopped; if strong, the resistance will not even be felt. The downswing of the wrist can also be resisted in the upper position, at the beginning of count two (Fig. 2-47). If fresh Ki is used to generate each movement, then the resistance is hardly even noticed. The Ki that goes up continues without turning back, to the ends of the universe. On count two fresh Ki comes down from above the clouds. There is no immediate connection between the Ki extended up and the Ki brought down. They are like two birds in flight, passing the same spot in opposite directions, moments apart.

The Secret of Mind and Body Coordination in Movement

Mind and body are essentially one, but they are governed by different principles, like bone and skin. The mind is without limit; the body is circumscribed by natural laws. Its limitations are far less restrictive than we ordinarily assume. The limits that most of us have learned to live with are not nature's limits; they are largely self-imposed. No one can fly like Superman, or catch bullets in their teeth. We can transport ourselves or avoid danger in other ways, without resorting to magic or fantasy. The mind is without limit; and that unlimited mind leads and controls our body. Simply believing this is not enough. We have to act as if we believed it were true. The Ki tests help us to test our natural doubts, and establish confidence in this basic principle. The moment we realize our belief in action, then our body does become stronger, more resistant to disease, transcending our own self-imposed weaknesses. The strength and skill which develops from this only seem like magic to the person who is still filled with self-doubt.

Every year, on the third of January, Ki Society students from all over Japan gather at the Kinugawa River in Tochigi Prefecture, for special cold weather training. Several hundred people, including many children, enter the chilly river water for several minutes; spending over an hour out-of-doors. The air temperature is usually well below freezing (Fig. 2-48). Ordinarily, conditions far less severe would be considered intolerable. But properly supervised by qualified people with Ki training, it is possible to enter the chilly waters without skipping a beat or catching cold.

The secret of coordinating mind and body in movement is to understand and apply the four principles of mind and body unification. Twenty principles have been given in this chapter for unifying the mind and body, in motion or at rest. Still it is essentially a simple process. The secret is this:

DO THE THING IN YOUR MIND QUICKLY,
AND RELAX COMPLETELY KNOWING THAT IT IS DONE.

Fig. 2-48

When you act strongly and assume that something positive is already accomplished, Ki extends very powerfully. Any further effort, especially physical tension and anxiety over results will cause you to violate the principles of mind and body unity, and will undo your strength. Call it positive thinking, faith, self-confidence, or what you will; but do not accept or reject this idea without giving it a fair test. Learn to coordinate mind and body through the exercises in this chapter, then experiment with the principles in your work and in your life.

The four basic principles of mind and body coordination have been explained in some detail, with applications to movement. Walking, rolling back and forth, boat-rowing, swinging the arm, turning and spinning, and swinging the hands are only a small sample of the Ki development curriculum. But they include a wide range of common everyday movements. They also illustrate how to develop a sense of rhythm, and how to keep one's balance under pressure, and in the midst of vigorous activity. These are valuable lessons to learn. If we do nothing else in life; to live, to survive, and to thrive in this world we must move. If we can move in a way that generates tremendous energy without upsetting our mind and body unity, then we can develop to our full potential as human beings.

3. KI Meditation

How to Sit in *Seiza*

In Japanese the word *seiza* (正座) is usually written with two characters, meaning "correct sitting." It refers to the traditional Japanese style of sitting on top of the ankles, legs folded under, and back erect. It is the posture typically assumed by *samurai* and people of the court in Japanese movies when sitting on the floor. For many people who have grown up sitting in chairs rather than on the floor, *seiza* is very hard on the knees. Even in Japan, today many people cannot sit *seiza* comfortably for long; and the posture is often considered excessively formal for daily life. Yet when the *seiza* posture is correctly assumed, with mind and body unified, it is both comfortable and powerfully stable. Using different characters, the same word *seiza* can be written to mean "quiet sitting," (静坐) which is closer to the spirit of Ki meditation.

Begin by kneeling on both knees, with the feet out flat behind you at right angles to the rest of the body, the right big toe crossed over the left. The knees are about two or three fist widths apart (Fig. 3-1). It is best to sit on a firm but slightly yielding floor surface, like a *tatami* mat, thick carpet, or multiply folded bath towel. Shake the wrists gently as in Fig. 1-7 to release tension from the upper body. However there is less bounce in the knees than there was in the ankles in the standing position. As the wrist motion becomes smaller, transfer the focus to the One Point.

With the index finger of one hand, touch the One Point on the lower abdomen (Fig. 3-2). Without exerting any pressure, gently push the One Point to the rear as far back as it will go, causing the upper body to lean forward, no more than 45 degrees (Fig. 3-3). Then gently lower the One Point as far down as it will go, without changing the forward leaning angle (Fig. 3-4). Next slowly straighten your upper body; only to the point where it feels to be about half-way between 45 degrees and straight vertical. In fact it will be more vertical than that, though it may feel like a slight forward bow. You will probably feel some residual tension in the shoulders, and in the thighs above the knees; so at this point swing both arms gently to release all stress from the body (Fig. 3–5). Finally place the hands palm down on the thighs, between the knees and the abdomen, at an inward angle of 45 degrees (Fig. 3-6). This is the *seiza* posture. It should feel both stable and comfortable, like riding high on horseback. The One Point is low and calm; and the lower back has a taut feeling. Viewed from the side, the spine forms a gentle S-curve, consistent with its correct anatomical position.

Fig. 3-1

Fig. 3-2

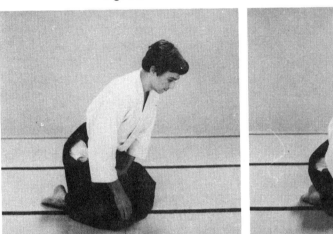

Fig. 3-3

Fig. 3-4

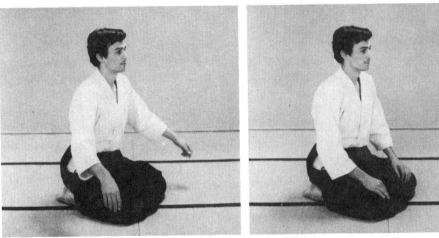

Fig. 3-5

Fig. 3-6

The rationale behind *seiza* becomes clear when it is compared to the basic standing unified posture. The part of the leg in direct contact with the floor, from the knee to the tip of the toes, is like a large foot. In the standing posture, the weight falls on the balls of the feet, not the heels. In the *seiza* posture, the weight also falls rather forward, not on the ankles. If the weight falls back on the ankles, *seiza* is neither correct nor comfortable. This can be caused either by sitting ramrod straight (Fig. 3-7), or by slouching (Fig. 3-8). Though either of these postures may feel comfortable at first, they cannot be maintained for long without having to adjust one's position. This is not "quiet sitting." Nor is it stable against any of the Ki tests. To be of any value, the posture used for Ki meditation should be stable against a variety of Ki tests.

Ask your partner to stand at your side, facing the same direction. Using the hand which is closest to you, he can test by pushing with the fingertips on the chest from the front (Fig. 3-9), or between the shoulder blades from behind (Fig. 3-10). If the posture is correct, it feels as solid as a rock; firm but without any sense of pushing back. This *fudôtai*, or immovable body is evidence of *fudôshin*, or immovable mind.

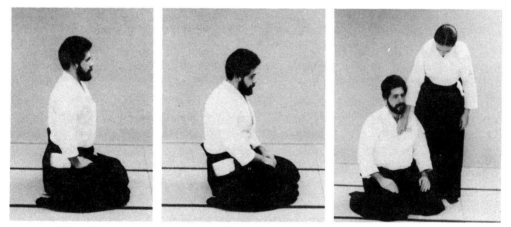

Fig. 3-7   Fig. 3-8   Fig. 3-9

Test the knee as in Fig. 1-10, being careful to lift straight up, and not lean in with full body weight (Fig. 3-11). The proof of the stability of *seiza* is found in comparing it to postures which are more rigid or more slack; not in doing everything in your power to shove or knock the person over. An elevator or an automobile can move anyone without a challenge. Ultimately, we are testing the unification of mind and body, not whether or not the body can be moved.

Ki tests are useful for verifying the level of mind and body unity. They can help us regain it when we lose it. The purpose of Ki meditation practice is to deepen that state; to root it so firmly in your subconscious mind that the winds of change and the crises of life no longer have the power to shake it loose. In this regard, the willow tree is often given as an analogy for *fudôshin:* unshakable roots deep in the ground, and a soft yielding resilience against the strong winds which blow through it.

Fig. 3-10   Fig. 3-11

Living Calmness and Dead Calmness

The word *meditation* is loaded with mental associations. Most of these are based on misguided assumptions about the nature of the mind and body. There are so many forms of meditation being taught, that it seems inappropriate to describe them all by the same word, Electro-encephalographic (EEG) readings on Yogic and Zen masters in meditation have clearly shown that they are not in the same mental state when they meditate. It is unreasonable to assume that all forms of meditation are simply "different paths to the same summit" as some people teach. As in the professions of Medicine or Law, there are many levels of competence and integrity in the world of meditation. Yet somehow people are more critical in evaluating conventional professionals than they are in selecting spiritual teachers.

Calming and focusing the mind at the One Point produces a strong degree of mental and physical strength. Contemplating one's navel does not. One stereotype of meditation is that it is a withdrawn, other-worldly state. Some people do cultivate this in their meditation practice; some make efforts to communicate with the dead, or leave the body. None of these practices are consistent with the principles of mind and body unification. In terms of Ki, these mental states are known as dead calmness. If you want to coordinate mind and body, it is best to avoid forms of meditation which cultivate separation of body and spirit. The aim of Ki meditation is living calmness: a state of unshakable calm while fully living in this world.

The *Mudra* of Mind and Body Unification

A *Mudra* is a hand gesture, assumed in a meditation posture, which has the power to achieve what it symbolizes. The *Mudra* of Mind and Body Unification is practiced in the *seiza* position. Interlocking the fingers in this *Mudra* instantly deepens the degree of mind-body unity. There is no compariosn between the stability of the body with and without this *Mudra*.

First assume the correct *seiza* position to unify mind and body. Turn your palms to your face and look at your fingertips (Figs. 3-12, 13). Slide the little finger of the left hand over the little finger of the right; doing the same for the next two fingers of each hand (Fig. 3-14) until the tips of the index fingers just touch. The tips of the smaller fingers also touch (Fig. 3-15). Slowly turn the palms to face each other, without letting the interwoven fingers come apart (Fig. 3-16). Turn the palms further out away from you; until the thumb of the right hand touches the base of the index finger of the left, and the thumb of the left hand lays across it to touch the base of the right index finger. The ball of each index fingertip should touch (Fig. 3-17). Turning the palms out, without letting the fingers come apart, stretches the little finger and ring finger the most. This produces subtle changes in the posture. The index fingers act like the nozzle of a hose; increasing and focusing the power of the Ki extended from the arm. Raise the tips of the index fingers to eye level (Fig. 3-18). This has the effect of stretching the little fingers and the lower back at the same time. The eyes may be left open or closed, but should be relaxed.

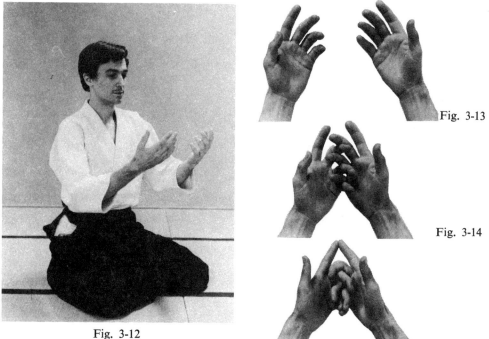

Fig. 3-12

Fig. 3-13

Fig. 3-14

Fig. 3-15

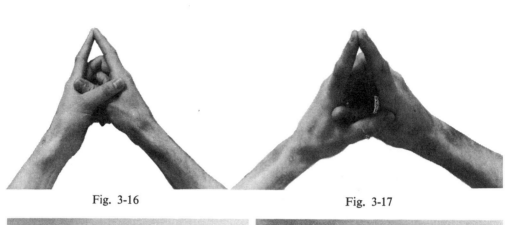

Fig. 3-16   Fig. 3-17

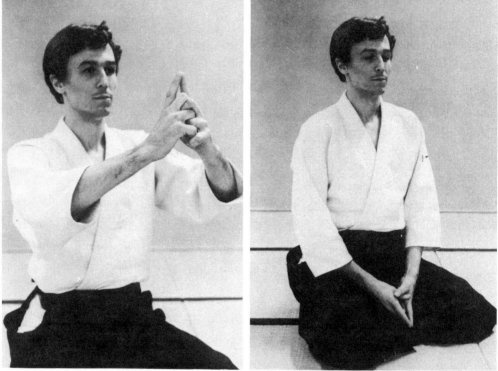

Fig. 3-18   Fig. 3-19

At first it may be difficult to maintain this position for more than a few minutes. But with practice it may be possible to extend the time to ten or fifteen minutes. As the arms get tired, the hands draw back closer to the face; which is acceptable as long as you maintain good posture. If you can endure the soreness and fatigue in the arms for a few minutes, somehow you find a second wind; and the arms feel light once again. Still in time, the arms become very heavy with fatigue. At this point, continue the meditation by letting the hands drop, as they are, into your lap

(Fig. 3-19). Because the arms are now totally relaxed as they fall, they may bounce once slightly off of your thighs before coming to rest. The arms may feel shorter than usual in this position, due to the shoulder joint being properly centered. Once the arms have recovered from the fatigue, you may raise them again to the eye-level position; alternating between the two positions as your endurance allows.

Though the arms may feel tired and sore in the raised position, that is when the benefits of the meditation begin to take hold. Bringing the hands closer to the face, or rotating the shoulders in place can help relieve the tension that may accumulate. But this is not the same kind tension that comes from failing to relax completely. It comes from the gradual toning and stretching of the muscles needed to support the arms in the correct position. Until you endure this discomfort, even for only a few minutes, and let the arms drop into your lap, you really cannot know the deeper meaning of complete relaxation and weight underside.

Sitting in *seiza* with the *Mudra* of unification gradually begins to effect subtle changes in your way of sitting, standing, and walking; though it may take some months of daily practice for the changes to become apparent. Considering the years of bad habits and physical malformations that you may have to overcome, several months is a relatively short time. As you practice Ki meditation in this posture, you will also notice improvements in digestion and metabolism, consistent with the repositioning of the abdominal organs which takes place. Mistaking collapsation for relaxation, many people have allowed their internal organs to sag under the excess pressure of misplaced upper body weight. Ki meditation will correct this condition, and restore vitality to many organic processes.

The deepening of the roots of mind and body which takes place in this posture are automatic and immediate, as long as the posture is correct. As in ordinary *seiza*, the chest, back, and knees can be tested for stability. The arms can also be tested by having your partner grab your index fingers and push straight down (Fig. 3-20). They should feel resilient and strong, like an automobile tire. The little fingers may also be pushed directly from the front (Fig. 3-21).

After you learn to sit in *seiza* with reasonable stability, you can attempt a more difficult Ki test. It is relatively easy to be stable against a test coming from a single direction. It requires a much deeper level of unification to pass a multi-directional Ki test. First unify the mind and body in the ordinary *seiza* position. Have your partner check your stability by trying to lift one knee (Fig. 3-22). If you pass that test, have your partner push on your chest from the front, using the hand that is closest to you, thumb down (Fig. 3-23). After passing both of these tests separately, try them both at the same time, with an equal or lesser amount of force (Fig. 3-24). This test is almost impossible to pass in the ordinary *seiza* position. In this case, one plus one equals a force of about five or ten. Testing from two directions at once magnifies the effect of the Ki test so much that it hardly requires any force at all to tip you right over. Now try the same two directional test in the same posture with the *Mudra* of unification (Fig. 3-25). It is many times more stable; so much so that it may be hard to beleive that your partner is testing with the same amount of force.

It is also interesting to compare the stability of this *Mudra* with that of the tra-

Fig. 3-20

Fig. 3-21

Fig. 3-22

Fig. 3-23

Fig. 3-24

ditional gesture of supplication; folded hands, in the *seiza* or kneeling position. Against any Ki test there is no comparison (Fig. 3-26). Most people pray and meditate with their spirit alone; completely forgetting to unify mind and body and meditate with the whole self. It is less effective to merely verbalize a prayer or positive affirmation without unifying mind and body. It may even have the reverse effect; because its ineffectiveness can shatter your faith or confidence.

The *Mudra* of unification can be very helpful during a difficult period or time of crisis. In unexpected and indirect ways, it can resolve a problem which seemed to have no easy solution; and is certainly worth more than an equal amount of time wasted in worry and confusion. Most of our problems, including those which seem beyond our control, can be traced somewhere to a loss of mind and body unity. If we can restore this, we regain the source of our strength. Some problems seem to be beyond our immediate control; such as a series of threatening phone calls from an unidentified stranger, or a traffic accident. But each of us plays a subtle role in our own misfortunes. Spending at least ten minutes a day in Ki meditation will lay the foundation for a time when you may need strength.

Fig. 3-25   Fig. 3-26

Principles of Ki Meditation

The *Mudra* of unification produces a deep state of mind and body coordination. However it is important to learn not to depend on a single form for meditation. There are occasions when you are with other people, or cannot draw attention to yourself by assuming an unusual posture. Perhaps you have to speak before a large group, or calm someone down in a heated argument. In such cases you must be able to quickly regain a deep state of composure, without behaving in a manner that would be misunderstood by the people around you.

Any posture in which mind and body are unified is suitable for Ki meditation. Whether standing or sitting, you may practice Ki meditation anywhere, provided that you have some experience of it in a seated posture. There are five principles for Ki meditation which clarify its real purpose.

1. Maintain a Posture of Mastery: A person who is master of a situation has no need to enforce or prove it. People willingly follow a person who is master of himself or herself. Such a person is a natural leader and friend to others. Being relaxed and extending strong Ki makes you master of yourself, and gives you the presence to master any situation.

2. Let Things Take Their Course: Letting things take their course is not the same as just letting things happen. There is a rhyme and rhythm to everything, and if we are calm enough we can see when to act and when to be still. Well meaning people often make a mess of things in their efforts to help out. Gain a tolerance for ambiguity, and you can see the wisdom of letting things take their course.

3. Create a State of Harmony: Simply by staying calm, you can help others to be calm. The reverse is also true; so we have a responsibility to create harmony in tense situations before they get out of control or erupt into violence. Rather than withdrawing into yourself, extend yourself calmly into the selves of those around you, and you will find it easier to create harmony in your dealings with other people.

4. Feel the Spirit of Life Animating All Creation: All things in the Universe are born of Ki and eventually return to it. The modern world has taught us to treat things as if they were dead, and only to see living things in terms of their usefulness. We need not follow any particular religion to feel fully alive. At the deepest levels, mind and body unification extends beyond the self to include unity with other people and the Universe itself.

5. Become Aware of the Movement of the Ki of the Universe: In Chapter 1, we defined Ki as, "a universal energy, capable of infinite expansion and contraction, which can be directed, but not contained by the mind." The ancient Chinese devised an elaborate cosmology to describe the circuits and pathways of this Ki; a system encompassing both acupuncture and astrology. While some of their insights were accurate, many were based on superstitions and social traditions which bear no relevance to contemporary Western society. Furthermore they are impossible to verify; so you are simply left to believe it or not, as you choose. However, though it appears that the sun goes around the earth, in fact it is not true. There is no need to stick to ideas just because they have been around for a long time. Moreover, Ki energy can be experienced and directed by the mind. Its movement is like the wind; invisible but powerful. Like the wind, Ki has rhythm. Like a hurricane, it gains power from its focus around a point.

Expansion and Contraction Meditation

The One Point is the center of the Universe. But the Universe has no definable limits; its center is everywhere and its circumference is nowhere. Relative thinking cannot comprehend infinity. That is why the mind cannot contain Ki. The very effort to hold, retain, and pin it down only weakens the flow of Ki in your body. If the Ki flow is severely restricted, you become sick. If it is cut off altogether, you die. In one sense our Ki is always returning to the Universe, so we need not fear death. Perhaps this is why some religions refer to death as liberation. But while we are alive we should fully participate in Life.

Sit in *seiza* with mind and body unified. Close your eyes and have your partner verify your stability with one or more Ki tests. Then have your partner test you again without warning, 30 seconds to a minute later. You may be disappointed to find that in that short time you lost your unified state, though you believed that you still had it. Despite our best intentions to keep the four basic principles, we usually lose them after a short period of time. Thinking about the One Point is a mental trick, devised to pin it down to a single spot. This is of course impossible, except in our imagination. People meditate for different reasons: to clear the mind, answer a problem, or gather their strength. The One Point can help you do all of these things. However, the moment that you think, "I've got it," you have already lost it. The evidence for this is that the eyelids begin to flutter slightly. When we dream our eyes make a similar motion, known as Rapid Eye Movement (REM). When we cut our Ki we also daydream. As our mind wanders, a subtle but important change comes over our face, one that may not be obvious to a person without Ki training. This change usually goes unnoticed by the daydreamer himself. It can easily be seen however in an exaggerated form, by closing the eyes and deliberately losing the One Point (Fig. 3-27).

Do not try to limit or contain the flow of Ki. Whatever direction it comes from, whatever direction you send it, let it go. Any change of direction should be led by fresh Ki, always coming from a distance beyond your conscious awareness.

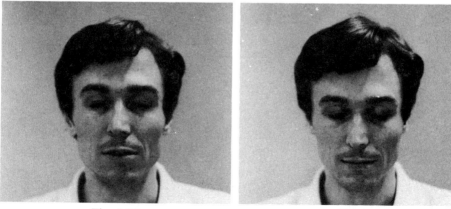

Fig. 3-27   Fig. 3-28

This amounts to living fully in the present, and having a positive attitude toward whatever you do. Think of the Ki energy condensing infinitely at the One Point. You may use an image, like shrinking by 1/2, 1/2, 1/2, . . . each successive moment. However the mind cannot follow this beyond a couple of seconds. It grows too small too fast. This is fine. Your eyes cannot follow an airplane to the end of its journey. Just because you can't see it doesn't mean that it doesn't exist. The beginning of Ki meditation is like starting an engine on a motorcycle. There is a rapid spin as the engine engages, then it is forgotten, though it is still running. Extend Ki vigorously, and let it go out of sight. You need do nothing more to maintain mind-body unity in Ki meditation. If you lose it, start again in the same way. Have your partner test you again, comparing the stability of the body when the mind lets go of Ki with when it tries to hold on to it. The same thing can be done with expansion meditation. Let the Ki expand rapidly out of sight, then just sit (Fig. 3-28). This is essentially no different than the secret of mind and body coordination in movement: do the thing in your mind quickly, and relax completely knowing that it is done. If you lose track of what you are doing, you can always start again anytime.

Strengthening Your *Seiza* Posture

There is an exercise, known as *Kokyû Dôsa*, which is performed by two people facing each other in the *seiza* position. While it appears to be a contest of strength, it cannot be won in a competitive state of mind. If your partner has mind and body unified, then even advantages of size and strength will be of little use. *Kokyû Dôsa* is an excellent way to strengthen your *seiza* posture for Ki meditation.

Sit in a unified *seiza* position, facing your partner in the same, with a distance of about one hand length between your partner's and your knees (Fig. 3-29). Extend your arms out at shoulder width, palms facing each other but slightly up, and elbows naturally bent (Fig. 3-30). Your partner reaches up to lightly hold your wrists from below and to the outside (Fig. 3-31). The object is to use Ki and move your arms to unbalance your partner, pushing him back or over to the side; without sliding your knees forward or standing on the toes for leverage until he is clearly off balance and on the way down. Do not move the arms until the One Point is fully forward (Figs. 3-32, 33). After he falls, the distance between you increases; and can be closed by sliding forward, and finally standing on the toes (Fig. 3-34). In the final position you are sitting on your heels; hands hovering lighlty above his chest, pinning him with Ki rather than physical pressure. Even once on his back, your partner should be unable to unbalance you by pulling or pushing on your wrists (Fig. 3-35). Your partner's object is to prevent all of this from the beginning; holding his ground without letting go of your wrists or sliding backwards. If your body is too tense, or your One Point too high, then your partner may push you back with his hands; even cause you to fall over (Fig. 3-36).

This exercise requires considerable practice, before you learn how to unbalance

Fig. 3-29

Fig. 3-30

Fig. 3-31

Fig. 3-32

Fig. 3-33

Fig. 3-34

Fig. 3-35   Fig. 3-36

your partner without relying on strength, speed, timing, or leverage. Such physical tactics are effective if your partner holds with strength, or lacks mind and body unity. However if your partner is unified, you will feel powerless to move him in this way. In your determination to throw your partner over, it is all too easy to lose your mind-body unity, and raise your hips, tighten your arms, stand up on your toes, or try some other trick of leverage. All of this pushes the weight upperside and makes the body tense, resulting in a helpless and impotent feeling.

The best way to succeed in unbalancing your partner is to unify yourself before you extend your arms, and before your partner becomes unified. Since *Kokyû Dô-sa* is not a wrestling match, there are no tricks of leverage. Developing muscular or torso strength will not make you any better at throwing a unified partner. It is best to work at first with someone of equal size, who has some understanding of mind and body coordination. Otherwise the exercise will degenerate into a mere contest, and have no value as Ki training. In time you should work with many partners. Everyone holds in a different way. All have something to teach you.

There are also various ways to increase the challenge of *Kokyû Dôsa*. If your partner pushes your wrists down with weight underside, rather than merely holding them, you may collide directly with his strength. He may push your wrists together, putting tension into your arms. There are tricks for throwing a partner who manages to move your wrists like this; but the best thing is to prevent their being moved in the first place. If you properly unify mind and body, the wrists cannot be easily moved up, down, or to the side. This is the fundamental form of *Kokyû Dôsa*.

If you have problems making progress with this exercise then make full reference to the Ki principles described in Chapter 2, dealing with how to move with mind and body coordinated. You may also break the exercise down into steps; doing Ki tests and asking your partner for feedback after every part of the move. Until the Ki principles are successfully applied, their power may not be obvious. However once their real meaning is discovered by either partner, the weaker partner's weight will float upperside like oil on water. There is no comparison between the stability of *seiza* with and without Ki.

4. KI Breathing

Blood, Breath, and Ki: Whole-Body Breathing

The ancient Chinese assumed that Ki entered the body through the breath, and flowed in the blood. They called this energy *Kiketsu* (気血), using the characters for Ki and blood. *Oketsu* (穢血), meaning dirty or polluted blood, was considered to be the source of all disease. Modern medicine uses a variety of blood tests to diagnose the health of the entire body, and the presence of many specific diseases. It is common knowledge that blood is the vehicle for oxygen, nutrients, and antibodies for every cell in the body.

Oxygen is the fuel which drives many of the processes of metabolism, including those which keep the blood composition clean and balanced. An abundant supply of oxygen, delivered to all of the cells of the body, is essential in retaining vitality, combating disease, and regenerating the body. In other words: blood, breath, and Ki are indeed closely related.

Yet the average person is almost literally starving for Ki at the cellular level. The reason is very simple: inadequate and shallow breathing, caused by a lack of mind and body unification. The average person takes about 16 to 20 breaths per minute, filling the lungs to about 400 cubic centimeters capacity. Yet in Ki breathing only one breath is taken per minute, filling the lungs to between 5,000 and 8,000 cubic centimeters capacity. Breathing in this way, eighteen times slower and at twelve to twenty times the capacity, an ample supply of oxygen and subsequent release of carbon dioxide is almost guaranteed.

In a square millimeter of subcutaneous tissue there are nearly 2,000 capillaries, all of which are open and circulating blood during Ki breathing, hard labor, and active sports. Yet in a state of rest, typically only about five of these capillaries contain blood, far less than one percent of capacity. "State of rest" is really a misnomer, because for most people this involves a state of literal collapsation; where the larger muscles may be in a state of flaccidity, but the deeper tissues are riddled with tension, due to inadequate support and poor distribution of the weight of the body. The diameter of a red blood cell is about four times that of a capillary, so that it must be squeezed through the thousands of miles of these micro-passages. All of this is accomplished quite naturally under hydraulic pressure, making one complete cycle around the body in little more than 20 seconds. In order to fully oxygenate and detoxify the blood, each inhalation should require at least 25 seconds, with the same amount of time for each exhalation, or about one breath per minute. Not only do most of us breathe at a fraction of the time and capacity ideally needed to clean the blood, but unclean air also contains pollutants which may hinder respiration even further.

In Japanese the word *naga-iki* (長息・長生) can be used synonymously to mean long breath and long life. An ancient story admonishes us that the number of breaths we may draw in our lifetime is pre-established; and that we should not use them up so quickly. When the mind or body are disturbed by anxiety or "disease," it is always reflected in shallow, inadequate breathing.

But it is not enough to simply fill the lungs to capacity through deep abdominal breathing. If the capillaries are largely closed off due to excess tension, then deep breathing has little meaning. The very effort to gulp massive amounts of air can cause the entire body to become tense. Some Oriental disciplines describe elaborate ways of "circulating" the Ki, especially as you hold your breath. This is poor advice, because holding the breath restricts the flow of Ki and introduces excess tension into the body. Ki circulates naturally when the mind and body are unified. In that natural state deep breathing has a profound effect, serving to both calm the mind and clean the blood.

Ki Breathing in the Standing Posture

Begin by standing in the unified posture. Raise the hand up to eye level, palm facing forward. This helps direct your attention to the head region. One-third of the oxygen in the body is consumed by the brain; so more time is devoted to the head region than to any other during exhalation. It is easier to learn Ki breathing through exhalation, so always begin breathing exercises by breathing out. Take a quick but not overfull in-breath before beginning the exhalation. Holding the hand at eye level, exhale for a full 15 seconds through the mouth (Fig. 4-1). Produce a "Hah . . ." sound with the breath, audibly and steadily, but without vocalizing.

It may be difficult at first to sustain a breath for this long. However if Ki is well extended before you begin, the posture is correct, and no excess tension grips the chest or neck, then it should be easy to exhale for 15 seconds. Although the sound is not vocalized, it helps to make it as open and "bright" as possible, more like a treble than a bass tone. Making the breath audible provides feedback on the movement of Ki. Because Ki and breath are so intimately connected, any disturbance in the continuity or flow of the breath is an indication of a similar disturbance in the mind or Ki. If the breath were not audible it would be very difficult to detect any such disturbance by yourself. Practice this 15 second exhalation until it becomes easy to complete, and still have a feeling that there is some air left over.

Next extend the breath another 5 seconds, making 20 seconds in all; slowly lowering the hand to chest level after the first 15 seconds, and drawing the attention down to the chest with the hand (Fig. 4-2). Imagine that you are emptying a large container, slowly draining it from the top down. During this 5 seconds, the "Hah . . ." sound may drop slightly in tone, though it is still not vocalized. Be careful not to let the shoulders sag or the chest collapse throughout the exhalation.

For the final 5 seconds, making 25 in all, and exceeding the time required for the blood to make one full cycle around the body; slowly lower the hand down to its resting position at your side (Fig. 4-3). During this 5 seconds, bend the neck forward at a comfortable angle. This helps to expel air remaining in the lungs, and better enables you to visualize emptying the container down to your toes. If you run out of air before the alloted time, just remain in this position, and imagine Ki flowing out in place of the breath. Even when the body stops moving the mind continues. Even though you can easily produce the "Hah . . ." sound for the full 25 seconds, keep the mouth open at the end and "exhale" Ki only for a few moments.

Inhalation is more difficult. But even if you only practiced exhalation, many of the benefits of Ki breathing could be realized. Nothing need be done to try to inflate or deflate the lungs. Relaxing the muscles which surround the lungs is the best way to let them expand and contract naturally. The process of exchanging gases with the atmosphere occurs automatically, through the capillaries which line the inside of the lungs. The best way to increase the lung capacity is to let the surface area of the lung tissue unfold and expand naturally. Whether or not mind and body are unified throughout Ki breathing can be verified with a Ki test.

When the exhalation is completed, gently turn the palm toward the front, thumb out. Begin inhaling slowly through the nose with the mouth closed, and the neck still bent forward. This time think of filling the body with air from the toes up, as if it were a container for liquid; taking 15 seconds to raise the hand to the navel (Fig. 4-4). If you inhale steadily, drawing Ki in from a point beyond the tip of

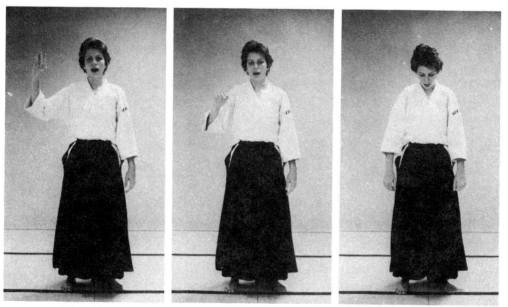

Fig. 4-1   Fig. 4-2   Fig. 4-3

Fig. 4-4   Fig. 4-5   Fig. 4-6

the nose, then 15 seconds should not strain your lung capacity. Imagine that you are smelling something fragrant. Though not necessary, the inhalation should produce a long, steady "sniffing" sound. It make take some months of practice before this sound appears. One day you will find that you can sustain it, at least for part of the inhalation. If you try to force the sound, you will fill the lungs too quickly and create tension in the shoulders.

For the next 5 seconds, raise the palm up to chest level, filling the container just as high, without yet raising the head (Fig. 4-5). In the final 5 seconds raise the head, and bring the hand back to eye level, palm facing forward (Fig. 4-6). If you fill your lungs to capacity before the time is up, just continue to "inhale" Ki in the place of air. Pause a few seconds, letting the movement of Ki continue, and repeat the process with another exhalation. Breathing exercises should both begin and end on an exhalation.

Ki Breathing in *Seiza*

The movement of the hand is useful in the beginning for understanding the process of Ki breathing. It is not necessary in ordinary practice. Standing may be more comfortable than *seiza*, but the *seiza* posture is ideal for Ki breathing. However, there are some differences in the movement of the upper body in *seiza*. The body remains in the upright position until the "Hah . . ." sound fades away, ideally at the end of 25 seconds (Fig. 4-7). Then the entire upper body, not only the neck, bends forward slightly about 20 to 30 degrees (Fig. 4-8). As in the standing position, the mouth is kept open until the end of the exhalation. Then the mouth is closed, and the body remains in this comfortable forward position until the end of the exhalation, another 25 seconds later (Fig. 4-9); after which it is brought back to the upright position (Fig. 4-10). After a pause, the next exhalation begins with strong Ki extension. In *seiza* as well, begin and end the exercise with an exhalation.

The exact time required to exhale or inhale is not important. Twenty-five seconds is offered as an approximate standard, which is almost certain to coordinate the circulation of Ki with that of blood and breath. If done in a unified posture, even a breath half that length will be beneficial.

Fig. 4-7

Fig. 4-8

Fig. 4-9

Fig. 4-10

Principles of Ki Breathing —————————————————

1. Don't Let the Air Leak Out, but Exhale with Purpose and Control: One purpose of the "Hah . . ." sound is to open the throat, lungs, and even the capillaries through relaxation. Another purpose is control. If the air is allowed to gush out it is difficult to sustain the exhalation for long. If the air is metered out in a discontinuous and choppy fashion, then the Ki is cut. The sound of the breath makes the movement of the Ki audible. The exhalation should be audible, but not loud. If it cannot be heard then it is difficult to tell if you are breathing properly.

2. Exhale with a Quiet, but Steady "Hah . . ." Sound: It is important that the breath be audible to yourself, but it need not be heard by someone in the next room. It is not a chant. There is a tendency to let the breath explode out at the beginning of the exhalation, and make a rather rough "Heh . . ." or "Huh . . ." sound. Though the breath should not be vocalized, no sound is as conducive to deep relaxation as "Hah . . . ." If the mind follows the breath and not the Ki, then the sound tends to become rough. If Ki precedes and leads the breath then the sound is calm and controlled, with a natural pause at the beginning and end of the breath.

3. Ki Continues on Forever where the Exhalation Leaves Off: Though the lungs have a limited capacity, Ki knows no such restrictions. Therefore our mind cannot grasp or contain Ki as it can the breath. This is why holding the breath does not cultivate strong Ki. It is not necessary to follow the movement of Ki to its end. Just watch it go out of sight as you would a sea bird disappearing in the distance.

4. Draw in the Breath from Beyond the Tip of the Nose, Until the Whole Body is Saturated with the Breath: It is easiest to lose mind and body unity at the moment of inhalation. Japanese swordsmen referred to this potentially fatal flaw as *suki*. A sigh is a good example of *suki*: the weight comes upperside, the chest and shoulders heave, or move up and down. Some people breathe as if they were sighing all of the time, mouth open and shoulders slumped. This is a sign of rough and shallow breathing, and of disease. In Ki breathing the Ki must precede and lead the breath.

5. Ki Disappears into the One Point where the Inhalation Leaves Off: Extend Ki and keep One Point are both principles of the mind. These two principles become one in the state of *reiseishin* (冷静心), or unshakable composure. It is easiest to find the One Point in stillness. Keeping it in movement is more difficult. But the most difficult by far is to keep the mind calm at the transitions between movement and stillness. When we stop one action and begin another; when we change direction; when we move from exhalation to inhalation; we tend to stop the mind. Follow the movement of Ki into the One Point, but don't try to stop or contain it there. After it disappears, just let it go and remain completely relaxed.

Benefits of Ki Breathing ───────────────────────────

Ki breathing should be practiced everyday, for from 15 to 30 minutes. In time, daily practice will produce many subtle and lasting benefits. You may find in six months, that you no longer catch colds, or have overcome some minor allergy problem. When done correctly, Ki breathing can improve all organic and meta- bolic processes. It improves the delivery of oxygen and nutrients, and accelerates the removal of toxins from bodily tissues. The liver and the kidneys are both close- ly involved in regulating and detoxifying the blood. They are both laced with capil- laries. Ki breathing makes them stronger and more efficient; resulting in improved health and resistance to disease.

It requires at least 15 minutes of correct Ki breathing to clean the blood. Most people devote far more time than that to washing their bodies; and yet devote no time at all to the more important task of cleaning the blood. We take care to wash our skin, but forget that the skin must also breathe. If the entire body is sprayed with paint, a person will suffocate. Ki breathing also improves the respiration of the skin. Like dental hygiene, daily practice is what produces lasting benefits. Thirty minutes a day of Ki breathing will produce a deep and unshakable state of mind-body unity in just a few years. It takes time to change the habits of a lifetime, but there is no better investment of your time. If you become sick or hos- pitalized, you should use the extra time to practice Ki breathing. If you have a serious health problem of any kind, you should practice from one to three hours per day, until you recover. If you are too sick to stand or sit up, you can practice lying down. It doesn't matter if you cannot sustain the breath for the full time. If you are too frail to practice inhalation, then just concentrate on exhalation alone. Even the attempt to do so will strengthen your body and speed your recovery.

Regular practice of Ki breathing will provide better emotional control and men- tal poise. It can overcome problems of anxiety and insomnia far more effectively and permanently than any form of drug or tranquilizer, without any harmful side effects. If you practice for at least 15 minutes before going to bed, your body will maintain the same slow, sustained breathing pattern all night long while you sleep. You will awaken truly refreshed. Ki breathing can enhance the effectiveness of napping or sleeping. Thirty minutes of Ki breathing before going to bed or upon waking is easily worth an extra hour of sleep. All of these benefits become evident with practice, though it may take some months for the effects to become notice- able. And still years later, daily practice will continue to unfold new benefits in physical and mental health. Daily practice is necessary, even if only for 10 minutes. If you wait for an emergency, or until you get sick, you will be too weak to make use of it. Skills and good habits are best formed under conditions without pressure. Shadow boxing prepares you for the real thing. But Ki breathing is also enjoyable enough to be its own reward.

Ki Breathing while Lying Down ─────────────────

Standing and sitting require some form of muscular support. An incorrect attempt to relax may result in a slouched posture, but not total collapse. However, lying down it is possible to totally collapse. Some forms of hypnosis make use of "progressive" relaxation, in which each part of the body is tensed, and released in turn, until the entire body feels limp and relaxed. This may have some appeal to a person who is exhausted from stress or fatigue, however it has no power to refresh the body or mind. A flaccid state violates all of the basic principles of mind and body unification. Though it may feel good, or may provide temporary relief to tired muscles; at best it only produces a dreamy and lazy state, and dulls important reflexes.

Lie down on your back, on a firm but comfortable surface such as a carpet. Try to capture the limp and relaxed state just described. Ask your partner to stand at your feet and lift them by the ankles. The result should be that your legs come up easily and your body bends at the waist (Fig. 4-11). A similar thing happens when you are lifted at the shoulders, though the upper body is somewhat heavier (Fig. 4-12). Both of these are signs of collapsed relaxation; the body's expression of a limp state of mind. This is of no use in Ki breathing.

To maintain mind and body coordination when you lie on your back, raise your hips slightly off the ground; and set them down again very lightly, as if setting a needle on a long playing record. The lower back, or "tail," will feel stretched and taut. After this, the rest of the body can be completely released. Maintaining this taut feeling, ask your partner to once again raise your ankles. Now the body should bend at the neck, and maintain its slight arch; a sign that Ki is strong (Fig. 4-13). The shoulders, on the other hand, may be almost impossible to lift, feeling heavy well beyond their proportion (Fig. 4-14). A unified mind and body has a tremendous capacity to absorb stress. Like a heavy bag of grain, it simply won't budge. But even if the shoulders are lifted, keep the lower back taut. Ask your partner to use the same amount of force as he used when the body was limp. If the test is fair, the shoulders will be much heavier in comparison.

If mind and body are coordinated, then Ki breathing can be practiced with good results, even in the supine position. Practicing while lying down is useful in falling asleep. It may be the only posture which you can use if you are ill. However it is not necessary to lean forward at the end of the breath, or to breathe for as long as 25 seconds. After some minutes it may be desirable to breathe both in and out through the nose. It is unhealthy to sleep with the mouth open, a symptom of weak Ki.

Whether taking a short nap or getting a full night's sleep, you can sometimes make yourself awaken refreshed at a certain time. Before you go to sleep, take note of the time. Quietly determine that you will wake up refreshed at an appointed time, or after so many minutes, and go directly to sleep. Your subconscious clock can be surprisingly accurate. Naturally there is no harm in setting an alarm clock to back you up if you cannot afford to oversleep.

Fig. 4-11   Fig. 4-12

Fig. 4-13   Fig. 4-14

Ki Breathing in a Group

You may wish to reinforce your discipline by practicing Ki breathing with a group of friends or family. The *seiza* position is best for group practice. Those who cannot sit in *seiza* may sit in a cross-legged position. While not strictly necessary, it is better if everyone exhales and inhales together. Some may be able to take longer breaths than others, so some compromise is needed to find a comfortable average length. The leader of the group should sit facing the rest. It is easy to tell when a person is nearly ready to begin a new breath, because he or she will lean slightly forward after each exhalation, and straighten up after each inhalation. The time to signal the new breath is when about half of the group members have completed an exhalation or inhalation. An effective way to signal this to the group is to clap two wooden blocks together (Fig. 4-15). The blocks should be longer than the hand, and fit comfortably in the palm. The type of wood is less important than the way in which the blocks are struck. A sharp crack-like sound is most effective at leading Ki. Strike the surfaces of the blocks together, parallel from a distance of about shoulder width. The blocks should be struck at about chest height (Figs. 4-16, 17). The best sound comes from moving with mind and body coordinated: do the thing in the mind quickly, and relax completely knowing that it is done. It takes practice to consistently produce the right sound. A good "Crack!" can act as a carrier for the Ki, giving the mind a fresh focus with each breath. A sharp

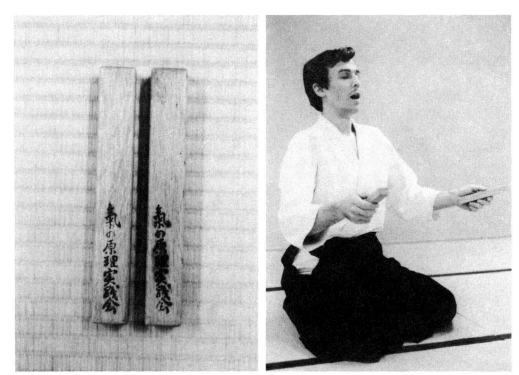

Fig. 4-15

Fig. 4-16

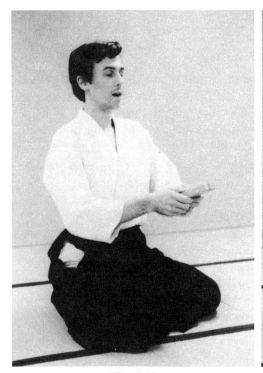

Fig. 4-17

Fig. 4-18

sound disappears quickly, but leaves the mind alert. A dull, or "double" sound, caused by striking the surfaces unevenly, is not an effective way to lead a group in Ki breathing; so some care should be taken to practice alone before leading a group.

The blocks are struck a moment before beginning the exhalation, and again before the inhalation, during the pause which separates each. During the rest of the breath the blocks are held at rest, comfortably in your lap; arms completely relaxed (Fig. 4-18). Be sure to pause a moment after hearing the sound before beginning to breathe, so that your mind can follow the Ki out of sight or into the One Point.

The final exhalation must also be signaled to the group using the blocks. There is a special rhythm to this final signal. The blocks are struck exactly 14 times within the length of the last exhalation, or about 25 seconds. The average length of the breath may vary from group to group; so the following rhythm is offered as a standard of time measurement. As asterisk (*) indicates a strike of the blocks; while a dash (–) indicates a silent mental pacing, which helps keep the Ki alive between strikes. One mark is given for each of the 25 seconds, although no numerical count should be made. Instead the sound should be followed as it cracks and disappears. The pattern is as follows:

   * _ _ _ * * * * _ * * * * _ * * * _ _ * _ _ _ _ *

In seconds, or numbers, it could be measured roughly as:

   1 – – – 5 6 7 8 – 10 11 12 13 – 15 16 17 – – 20 – – – – 25

The silence which follows the final crack of the blocks should not be disrupted immediately by trivial remarks. Careless behavior tends to cut the Ki and undo the effect produced by the wooden blocks. The rhythm is measured, but not mechanical. Its unhurried pace carries over into the activities which follow the breathing session.

Kiai

The Japanese word kiai (氣合) is sometimes translated as yell or shout. Kiai does involve a projection of the voice, made famous by actors in Oriental martial arts films. However the word kiai literally means a unification or joining of Ki. In this sense even a silent kiai is possible. Any projection of the voice with Ki is kiai; whether loud or soft, spoken or shouted. The secret of kiai is to extend Ki strongly before you speak, and don't interfere with the voice by tensing the throat.

Parents and teachers repeatedly scold children, and then complain that their words "go in one ear and out the other." Actually, in most cases their words never went in at all. If there is no Ki to give the words penetrating power, then the words have no impact. It does no good to react to a child's behavior with a mind which itself is shallow and upset. Not being able to control themselves, most adults have no ability to control or gain respect from children or young people. Whether scolding a child, telling a story to a friend, or giving a speech; coordinate mind and body before you open your mouth. Then your words will have maximum impact.

Fig. 4-19

Kiai can be focused by making a sound while visualizing a penetrating image. The sound "ee-yay-ee! . . ." is very effective in focusing penetrating Ki through an object. The sound arises from the lower abdomen, expands, and then sharply focuses again, like a long tapered lens (Fig. 4-19). If you practice without relaxing completely, then it will only give you a sore throat. Don't overdo *kiai* practice or you will strain your voice. Volume is not the objective. The purpose of *kiai* is purification and mind-body unity in an instant. The sound can be very sharp and penetrating, like an arrow. Feel the movement of Ki like a strong gust of wind passing through you and beyond. Let the voice be swept into it. The silence which follows good *kiai* is audible. Don't disturb it with trivial talk or movement. Take *kiai* practice seriously, and you may develop the ability aquired by legendary *samurai,* who could use *kiai* to stop a person in his tracks.

PART II

Ki Development
in
the Japanese Arts

5. SHODÔ: *Brush Calligraphy*

Life and Death in the Brush

It is not necessary to be able to read Chinese characters to appreciate their beauty or expression of Ki. *Shodô* (書道), or brush calligraphy, is like a visual form of music. The structural balance of the character, the rhythm and beauty of the lines do not depend on the meaning of the character. However, calligraphy is more abstract than *sumie* ink painting, which has gained more popular attention in the West. As an art form in itself, *Shodô* has its own principles and techniques, but it can also be used as a refined method of Ki development.

Kaisho: Printed-Style Calligraphy

The style of calligraphy which most clearly reveals the structure of the character is known as *kaisho* (楷書). Though it is formed in a printed style, it is handwritten with a soft brush. The spacing of the strokes within a character, and of the characters in relation to each other on the page is a matter of experience and judgment. If any of the beginning strokes or characters are made too large, too small, or drawn out of position, then the balance of the entire composition will be thrown off. One of the most important elements in *kaisho* is the expression of expanding space within the very strict limitations of the page and the large number of strokes which must be represented (Fig. 5-1).

This sense of expansion is impossible to achieve in type-set characters (Fig. 5-2). Type-set characters are basically limited to parallel vertical, horizontal, and diagonal stokes. They are too rigid and uniform to create a sense of expansion. But brush strokes drawn by hand are soft and flexible, like living branches on a tree. If you closely observe the strokes which seem to be parallel, it becomes apparent that they diverge at very subtle angles. If the strokes are completely parallel, they lack life; like type-set characters. But if the angle of divergence between the strokes is too obvious, then it destroys the sense of stability and strength in the character.

The strokes are laid down in a certain order, with rather strict limits on relative proportion (Fig. 5-3). Thousands of years of experience have established rules for the most efficient stroke order. Though drawn on a flat surface, the natural overlap of the strokes suggests a three dimensional structure, almost lifting the character off of the page. The ends of the strokes are often tapered or fluted, giving them a

Fig. 5-1

Fig. 5-2

Fig. 5-3

Fig. 5-4

Fig. 5-5

Fig. 5-6

"Through the old, we understand the new."

more natural appearance, like that of bamboo stems and leaves. Care is taken to preserve the character of individual strokes, even when they join and overlap with others. This gives even further depth to the space inside the character.

The brush is so sensitive to the slightest tremor in the hand, that it immediately registers any disturbance in the mind. It takes many months of practice to be able to consistently paint *kaisho* strokes properly. Within each stroke is a center line, representing the actual movement of the center of the brush (Fig. 5-4). This is essentially a Ki line, mostly drawn in the mind with a very steady hand. The brush is so soft, and contains so much ink, that any attempt to consciously drawn this Ki line with the body will produce an absurd exaggeration of the desired effect. The brush magnifies the centrifugal force of the hand many times. In this sense the brush acts like a lie detector test, clearly registering any disturbance in your mind as you write. Merely keeping the brush steady is no answer, for it only takes the life out of the stroke. Though not often taught as such, the secret is to draw the Ki line strongly in the mind, maintain good posture, and relax the arm completely to let the brush express itself.

Byô-hitsu (病筆) are strokes which are sick or deformed. They are often symptomatic of disease, carelessness, and a rough state of mind. People who become easily distracted or upset often write vertical, horizontal, and diagonal strokes which seem to twist or change direction (Fig. 5-5). This is a sign that Ki extension is weak and lacking direction. People who are careless and insensitive tend to show it in the weakly tapered beginnings and endings of their brush strokes (Fig. 5-6). Stroke deformities become more obvious when seen side by side with healthy strokes (Fig. 5-7). Most of these distortions are the result of tension in the body, which causes the brush to waver and produce exaggerated strokes, lacking subtlety and power.

Though some of the distortion is due to lack of practice or knowledge of how to use the brush, handwriting is often a sensitive barometer of Ki extension. A healthy person can easily visualize and express the expansive sense of space within and around the characters. A person who is ailing, mentally or physically, usually

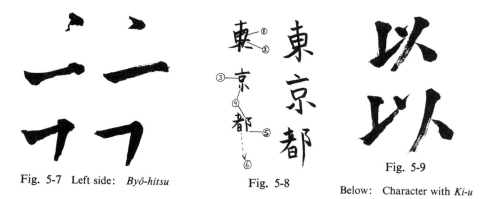

Fig. 5-7 Left side: *Byô-hitsu*

Fig. 5-8

Fig. 5-9

Below: Character with *Ki-u*

shows it in his handwriting. Japanese is often written vertically, read from top to bottom, right to left. In a healthy individual's handwriting, the characters stay on or close to the centerline, like a car staying on the road. Proper spacing and timing is observed in the laying down of strokes, so that there is no sense of hurry, no near misses, collisions, or other signs of lack of control. One sign of tightness (Fig. 5-8) is converging strokes which should be parallel (1). Another sign of tension is crossing strokes which should only touch (2). A sick person tends to close up and create narrow spaces where it should be open (3)-(4), as if the character itself were unable to breathe freely. Momentary lapses in concentration produce strokes which are prematurely curtailed (5). Sickness makes the body tense, causing the characters to gradually veer off to the right toward the bottom of the line (6).

Unlike the expansive strokes shown in good *kaisho* brushwork, these *byô-hitsu* seem to turn in on themselves, like shriveled dead leaves. Good calligraphy looks bigger than it actually is, and leads the mind beyond itself. The hand of a sick person seems tied in knots. In extreme cases, *byô-hitsu* can be a sign that the person has become dangerously accident prone.

The term *Ki-u* (気宇), literally meaning Ki universe or space, is used to refer to the internal space of the character. This is not merely a function of distance; because if the parts of the character are drawn too far apart, it seems loose and illegible. *Ki-u* means broad-mindedness, not lack of coherence. Characters drawn with *Ki-u* seem ready to burst, like ripe fruit (Fig. 5-9). While lack of *Ki-u* may be a sign of weakness, it is not necessarily a prognosis of disease. Like a seismograph, the brush picks up tremors in the hand. These tremors are very subtle early-warning signs of trouble or disturbance in the mind and body. *Shodô* training makes a person more alert to these signs. By copying masterworks of *Ki-u*, the student begins to relax and extend Ki naturally. This primes the wellsprings of life, and corrects the problem before it ever gets serious.

Gyôsho: Semi-Cursive Calligraphy

While the most outstanding feature of printed-style calligraphy is its command of space, semi-cursive *gyôsho* (行書) has an impelling sense of rhythm. *Gyôsho* is a freer hand, more likely to express the personality of the individual. The secret to a good sense of rhythm is the ability to express calmness in motion, and vitality at rest; a natural expression of mind and body coordination. The *ki-myaku* (気脈), or pulse of Ki, is evident in the stroke order, made partly visible by the trails of ink which connect the strokes (Fig. 5-10).

The strokes in *gyôsho* delicately overlap and fold into one another. The subtle path of the brush is easier to trace in an outline drawing (Fig. 5-11). Some strokes are run together, without lifting the brush from the page. The brush lightly licks the surface of the paper causing the line to swell and fade as the brush rises, falls, and turns. The stem of the brush is held vertically, but the hairs of the brush flex and fold freely. If the brush is held with Ki, then the tip of the brush trails powerfully down the centerline of each stroke. Most *kaisho* strokes appear basically straight. But *gyôsho* characters are written with strokes that curve. Their vitality comes from a sense of resistance to the curve; a tautness like that in a drawn bow. The direction of this curve is not random. Horizontal strokes usually curve upwards; vertical ones curve to the left or right (Fig. 5-12). This is due to the centrifugal force which springs from the dynamic rhythm of the *gyôsho* brush. *Kaisho* reveals the architectural beauty of space; *gyôsho* more often that of asymmetrical balance and rhythm.

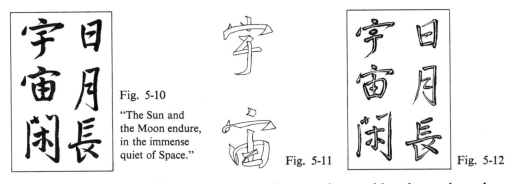

Fig. 5-10

"The Sun and the Moon endure, in the immense quiet of Space."

Fig. 5-11

Fig. 5-12

In *gyôsho* it is acceptable to run some strokes together, making the stroke order more apparent. However convention dictates that only certain kinds of stroke liasons are permissible. Still, *gyôsho* is written with a quick and sometimes carefree hand, making it easier for unconscious habits and personality traits to come out in the handwriting. Whereas *kaisho* strokes reveal the lines of the character; *gyôsho* strokes reveal the lines of the heart. Personality variations and idiosyncrasies are apparent in the way that the individual strokes are connected. Conventionally, the liaison should be made with a tapering stroke which may or may not touch the next stroke. However people who are particularly bold, active, and confident will tend to connect most or all of their strokes, using rather heavy lines (Fig. 5-13). Thin but continuous connecting strokes suggest a sense of grace and delicacy (Fig. 5-14). People who put a stem on the end of every stroke without connecting any of them, tend to be nervous types; the kind of person who clears his throat before speaking, or constantly combs his hair (Fig. 5-15).

Once the basic strokes of *kaisho* are mastered, it becomes possible to develop *Ki-u*; the internal space of the character. The next step is to express and develop a sense of rhythm in movement. Once you learn to unify mind and body in a static posture; the next step is to learn how to coordinate mind and body in movement. Rhythm, and a dynamic sense of balance in daily life are the real benefits of learning to paint *gyôsho* calligraphy.

Fig. 5-13   Fig. 5-14   Fig. 5-15

Sôsho: Cursive Calligraphy

If *kaisho* shows the lines of space, and *gyôsho* its rhythm, then *sôsho* (草書), or cursive calligraphy is perhaps best suited for showing the Ki lines of space. *Sôsho* is written in a running hand, without stopping (Fig. 5-16). Breaks between the strokes are the exception rather than the rule. Most modern Japanese cannot read *sôsho* without special training in calligraphy. Still, cursive calligraphy is not merely a free-style scribbled hand. Its rhythms are close to the universal rhythms of Ki. There is rhythm in the spacing and size of the characters, as well as in the contrasts of wet and dry strokes. Yet each column is subtly knit by a falling vertical line which penetrates the center of each character. The characters breathe independently in their own space, yet flow one into the next, as if written in one continuous stroke. Yet these are relative qualities, which can be infinitely developed and refined.

The outline of *sôsho* strokes resembles that of *gyôsho*, but it is more abbreviated and dynamic (Fig. 5-17). The brush often delicately retraces its own path, traversing the stroke it has just created at a minutely different angle, before firmly branching out in a new direction. It is impossible to write good *sôsho* without first mastering the more structured forms of *kaisho* and *gyôsho*. The carefree movement of the brush is really an optical illusion; and one which is very difficult to reproduce in practice. The subtlety of *sôsho* conceals its underlying structure, without which it is no more than mere scribbling.

Sôsho strokes are considerably abbreviated, as can be seen in the centerline of the brush movement. The subtlest movement creates a large effect, because the brush is alive in the hand. A fully relaxed hand produces a whip-like motion; the centrifugal force of the weight underside in motion. Use of a fuller portion of the brush creates a dynamic variation in the thickness of the line. The brush apparently moves without stopping; but actually its flow is punctuated by pauses, which seem to accumulate and release energy in each next stroke.

Although *sôsho* originates from a form of lettering more primitive than *kaisho*; comparing the two side by side makes it evident just how far the characters have

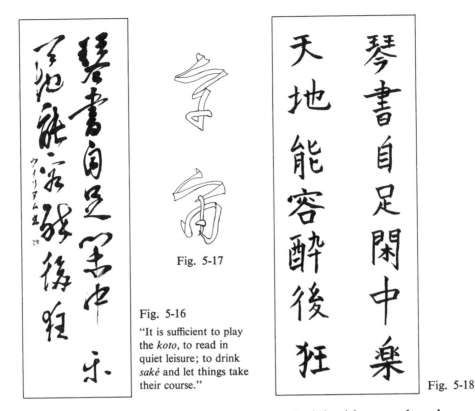

Fig. 5-17

Fig. 5-16

"It is sufficient to play the *koto*, to read in quiet leisure; to drink *saké* and let things take their course."

Fig. 5-18

been abbreviated (Fig. 5-18). Several strokes may be joined into one broad sweep, giving only a suggestion of the full structure. Yet to a trained eye, it is an intelligible form of handwriting. A good calligrapher can easily tell the difference between *sôsho* and merely rapid or sloppy writing. The difference is partly a matter of writing within the range of acceptable forms; but mostly a matter of the life energy which invigorates the brush strokes.

Sôsho contains within itself the structural possiblities of *kaisho* and the rhythmic sense of *gyôsho*. But it is closer to the spirit of Ki than either one. It is fluid and free, like running water; but it is legible. Likewise, the movement of Ki in the Universe is beyond our grasp, but somehow within our experience. More important than learning to read the script, is learning to read the Ki within and between the lines. Perhaps as Westerners gain a greater appreciation for Ki, then *Shodô* will gain greater recognition and appreciation in Western countries.

"The character is a picture of the soul."

We have already seen examples of how weakness in a person's character or health are reflected in handwriting. Character strengths come out just as clearly. Furthermore they can be cultivated by copying masterworks by individuals of great character or Ki strength. It is impossible to copy them accurately without at least temporarily assuming the same frame of mind. Individuals who have been well trained

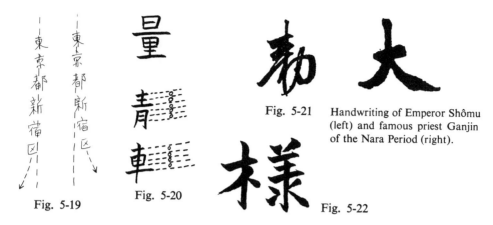

Fig. 5-19

Fig. 5-20

Fig. 5-21 Handwriting of Emperor Shômu (left) and famous priest Ganjin of the Nara Period (right).

Fig. 5-22

in the martial arts, tea ceremony, or other disciplines requiring deep spiritual concentration often produce very straight vertical columns of calligraphy. This is difficult to do because it requires an unbroken concentration; encompassing the whole line, both above and below the character now being written. A weaving or slightly meandering vertical line is often produced by people who enjoy quick mental and physical reflexes. Their adjustments to the vertical are smooth, not jagged. Lack of concentration produces lines which veer off to the right or left as they near the bottom of the page (Fig. 5-19). A person whose handwriting shows an organized disposition of internal space by evenly spaced parallel lines is probably a good organizer, and in good health as well (Fig. 5-20). Well protruding vertical strokes have been found in the calligraphy of great Japanese leaders and statesmen, perhaps suggesting leadership or independence (Fig. 5-21). People who write brush strokes with a well-defined beginning and end are generally very stable individuals, responsible, and good at follow-through (Fig. 5-22).

Shodô paintings are like pictures of the subconscious mind. They are not final statements, but rather instant snapshots of the personality at the time of writing. That personality can be developed and strengthened through Ki practice. On the other hand, careless calligraphy is also a form of practice; reinforcing bad habits and stunting the growth of the personality.

"Master Kôbô can paint well with any brush."

Master Kôbô Daishi, also known as Kûkai, was a Buddhist Priest who lived in ninth century Japan. Among his many talents, he was famous for being able to produce marvelous calligraphy with totally ordinary materials. He taught that when the brush is raised, it should be fully rooted in *Konton Kaiki* (混沌開基), or the mysterious origin of all things; the Universe. As a result of his profound state of mind and body unity, he was able to transcend the limitations of tools and techniques, and write directly from the spirit. Technology and tools have gradually come to replace human spirit and ingenuity in solving many kinds of problems. As necessary as this may have been, and as many blessings as it may have produced, it has probably also weakened our original state of mind and body coordination. When the game of golf was invented in Scotland hundreds of years ago, players used only a single club for all shots, from long drives to putts. No doubt, this required a great deal more of the player in terms of mind and body coordination than does the modern game.

Before you can master the art or the tools, you must first master yourself. This means painting with Ki; with the whole mind and body.

Kôbô Daishi was the founder of the Jubokudô school of calligraphy in ninth century Japan. The word *Jubokudô* (入木道) literally means, "Penetrating Wood Way." It came from the fact that the school's founder could paint on a piece of wood, causing the ink to penetrate so deeply that the characters could not be sanded off; as if the characters themselves, and not just the ink, had penetrated deeply into the wood. In the *Hagakure*, a medieval *samurai* classic text, warriors were advised to shatter the paper with the brush when they wrote. This did not mean to tear the paper, but rather to penetrate it deeply with their Ki.

A truly penerating character will literally grip the thin paper on which it is painted; causing faint wrinkles to radiate out from many of the strokes (Fig. 5-23). The centerline of Ki literally binds the stroke together from within. But mind-body unity must be maintained before and after painting the stroke as well, if it is to be genuine. Throughout the entire process of preparing the ink, on through to the washing of the brushes and inkstone, if Ki is cut at any point along the way, it will tell in the strokes. Even a calligrapher with considerable technical proficiency can benefit from Ki training in this way. Particularly important is the moment just after the character has been painted. After the brush leaves the page, there is a lingering moment where the brush may be poised in the air (Fig. 5-24).

Fig. 5-23
"Ki"—written in a fully cursive *Sôsho* style.

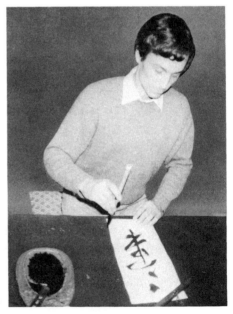

Fig. 5-24

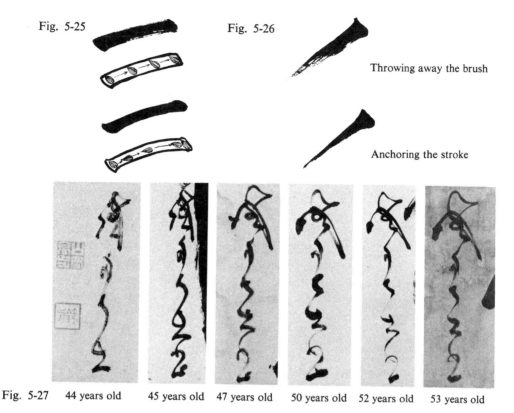

Fig. 5-25

Fig. 5-26

Throwing away the brush

Anchoring the stroke

Fig. 5-27   44 years old   45 years old   47 years old   50 years old   52 years old   53 years old

That the stroke is bound together from the inside, is technically a function of drawing the brush tip down the center of the stroke. It is also possible to move the brush with the tip on the outside edge of the stroke, though the effect is a weaker one (Fig. 5-25). If the tip trails down the center, it produces a bold, front-facing stroke, in which all of the hairs of the brush gather and focus at a point. If the brush tip is dragged along the outside, it produces a weaker, side-facing profile.

Though the brush strokes are drawn with dynamic movements, there must be control to the very tip of the stroke. If the stroke is merely drawn quickly, then the ending will be weak. This is known as throwing away the brush. In order to be able to enter the next stroke with equal Ki and control, the ending of the stroke must be gently anchored (Fig. 5-26). This comes about naturally from the sudden change of direction. If too much effort is made to consciously anchor the stroke, then it will leave a heavy and dead feeling in the stroke.

Yamaoka Tesshû (1836–88) became the fifty-second headmaster of the Jubokudô school of calligraphy. One of the most prolific calligraphy masters in Japanese history; he allegedly produced over one million works of art in the last eight years of his life! He was also a sword master of great renown. The secret of his tireless energy was Ki: "Gather all things in Heaven and Earth in your brush, and you will never tire."

The development of Ki over years of hard training is quite evident in Tesshû's signature during the last nine years of his life (Fig. 5-27). The Ki in his brush strokes gradually gained depth and maturity, as well as strength. Tesshû experienced enlightenment at the age of forty-five, and died at the age of fifty-three. The change in his character after his enlightenment is evident in the way that his signature hangs upon the vertical line. Though the centered quality of the signature is best grasped intuitively, it can be roughly measured by a transparent ruler, using the center of the stroke at the bottom of the signature as a baseline. The beauty of the balance is paticularly evident in the signatures drawn at age forty-five, soon after his enlightenment, and at age fifty-three, soon before his death. The increase of *Ki-u*, or internal space, is also evident at the top of the signature.

The binding of the stroke from within is perhaps more evident in the trails of ink particles left by Tesshû's brush, as viewed under an electron microscope (Fig. 5-28). What began as a diffuse and dispersed wake of ink particles, over time became a razor-sharp line of particles, practically spinning off of each hair of the brush in single file. This is not a matter of merely writing faster. Furthermore, it cannot be faked. As reliable and unique as a fingerprint, microscopic analysis has been used to identify authentic Tesshû originals from the many counterfeits that were produced. It is impossible to paint strokes like this unless every hair of the brush is infused with Ki energy.

Fig. 5-28   **a.**   37 years old
               b.   45 years old
               c.   47 years old
               d.   50 years old
               e.   52 years old

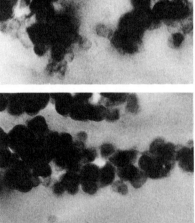

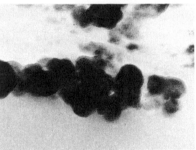

The ancient Chinese designated a point in the lower abdomen as *Kikai* (気海): literally, ocean of Ki. A person's Ki was considered to emanate from this point, through the nerves all over the body, and out into the world, where it joined with the Ki outside in *Kiai*. When *Kiai* is strong, there is little or no distinction between self and the world. In the martial arts, *Kiai* usually refers to the projection of Ki through the voice. Strong *Kiai* exerts a pressure strong enough to temporarily immobilize or control a person in his path. A silent *Kiai* is used in *Shodō*. The explosive extension of Ki, focused by the image and lines of the character, meets the paper with a soft and relaxed hand. If successful, then Ki itself draws the character; presenting you with what is known in Zen as "the original face, before you were born."

Shodō and Ki Development

With a little practice and care, anyone can learn to produce respectable hand-writing with a sharp pencil. The pencil is stiff and easy to control. The brush how-ever leaks ink as it touches the page. It is soft and flexible, like a whip, and regist-ers any and all influences upon it. A rigid writing instrument is like a tricycle, stable and easy to control. The brush is more like a bicycle, or even a unicycle. It takes practice and a good sense of balance to control the brush; but even that is not enough to perform difficult maneuvers. There is no erasing in calligraphy; no way to cover your mistakes.

The brush itself acts like an inkwell absorbing ink all the way to the stem; enough to write several characters in a row. The ink is drawn into the center of the brush by hundreds of tiny hairs; which must be gathered to a point, so that the ink may flow out smoothly. If the ink is carelessly sponged up, then it leaks out too fast, or even drips on the paper. If there is too little ink, it allows air to come between the hairs at the top of the brush, and weakens the draw of ink; causing the brush to run dry before the character is completed (Fig. 5-29). A desir-able dry-brush effect can be created by moving the brush quickly, or by using a brush with stiffer hairs. If this effect is not overdone, it gives the stroke a three dimensional, branch-like quality, as if it was alive. And yet it should still be pos-sible to paint wet strokes after the dry ones, without having to dip the brush for more ink. The point is control.

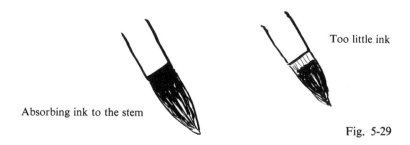

Too little ink

Absorbing ink to the stem

Fig. 5-29

Since *Shodô* requires hours of practice, over many years, it is easy for beginners to become distracted or bored. This is immediately apparent to a good teacher, who notices the changes in posture and breathing. Sometimes it is not enough to be told, so the teacher may test the student by suddenly pulling up on the end of the brush. If the student is concentrating properly, and visualizing a correctly drawn character, the fingertips grip the brush handle with Ki, and the brush doesn't move (Fig. 5-30). However the brush cannot be held too tightly, or it will be impossible to move the arm smoothly. Tension destroys mind and body unity. More often the student is caught daydreaming, with only a poorly formed image of the character in mind. In this case the grip is too loose, and the brush slips right out of the hand, leaving the fingers wet with dripping ink (Fig. 5-31). This same Ki test can easily be done with a pencil.

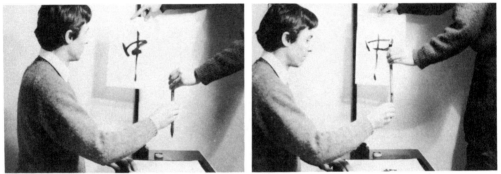

Fig. 5-30   Fig. 5-31

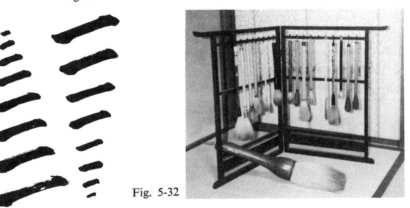

Fig. 5-32   Fig. 5-33

Even a very good copy of a masterwork will look different when seen from a distance. The cuts in the flow of Ki, and points where control of the brush was lost become more apparent in the perspective of distance. The best way to remove these cuts, or lapses in concentration, is to begin extending Ki well before you begin painting. It is particularly important to extend Ki during the preparation of the ink and practice itself, as well as after finishing; even while washing the brushes. Otherwise your actual period of Ki training is too limited, and too inhibited by the difficulty of mastering new techniques. Whatever objects we hold in daily life, we should hold in this way.

Ki is capable of infinite expansion and contraction. This was explored in Ki meditation, using the image of 1/2, 1/2, 1/2, ... A similar kind of Ki meditation can be performed with the brush, writing a single stroke many times in a vertical column, each one smaller than the one before; and then expanding the stroke back to its original size (Fig. 5-32). Much the same thing happens when writing on spaces of different sizes and shapes. Whether writing on a postcard, a fan, or a scroll, each field of space poses its own unique limitations. When the mind is calm, these boundaries, and the dynamics of their internal space become quite clear.

Brushes are made in a variety of sizes (Fig. 5-33). A large brush requires you to move your whole body, perhaps even straddling the page. Within a certain range, small brushes can be used to write large characters, and the tip of a large brush can be used to write small characters. Variation in materials and size of the space presents different challenges.

Implications for Daily Life

Ours is a visual society, and we are constantly shaped by subtle visual influences in our environment. Most of these are fragmented and negative in content, and very few of them are consciously chosen. One need only look at the posture of a person watching television to see what effect a random barrage of images has on a person's Ki.

Fig. 5-34

Fig. 5-35

Fig. 5-36

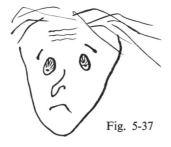

Fig. 5-37

Whether positive or negative, even simple images have an immediate effect on our Ki. Sit with good posture, and extend one arm out palm down, parallel to the floor. Have your partner push down on your wrist with his fingertips, just lightly enough to be sure that there is some resistance or spring in your arm. Perform the test while looking at a drawing of a smiling face, or some other postive image (Figs. 5-34, 35). The result should be strength and resilience in the arm. Now repeat the test again while looking at a drawing of a sad face, or some other weak image (Figs. 5-36, 37). Though you try to keep the arm up as before, it should be noticeably weaker against the same test. Some extremely negative pictures apparently have the power to rob the arm of any resistance at all. The impact of the image is immediate, if temporary. Ki training will strengthen you against the influence of negative images. The facial expressions, postures, and gestures of the people that you surround yourself with, all have a powerful visual impact on our subconscious mind.

Fig. 5-38   Fig. 5-39

The characters and brush strokes drawn by the human hand somehow recall the postures and forms of the human body. The same Ki test can be performed on the arm looking at a character that lacks any vitality (Fig. 5-38); and looking at one which is strong and balanced (Fig. 5-39). Students of *Shodô* spend many hours looking at and copying masterworks of calligraphy, drawn by their teacher, or by masters of many centuries past. It is commonly assumed that association with refined works of calligraphy has a beneficial influence on the character of the student. But the real benefits of *Shodô* begin when the student notices the elements in his own handwriting which lack *Ki-u*, rhythm, and vitality, and begins to make efforts to correct them. This initiates changes in the subconscious mind, which eventually become apparent in the way the student approaches daily life. *Ki-u* in the handwriting reflects broadmindedness in the soul. As the mind opens itself to life, then the exchange of Ki with the universe becomes more and more vigorous, resulting in improved health and physical circumstances as well, making *Shodô* a marvelous and sophisticated form of Ki development.

6. AIKIDÔ: *The Way to Union with KI*

The Way to Union with Ki

Aikidô means the "Way to union with Ki" or the "Way to harmony of the spirit." It was developed in this century as an art of self-defense and spiritual training. The word *Ai-Ki-Dô* comes from three characters (Fig. 6-1). *Ai* means to fit, harmonize, or agree with. The top three strokes were originally joined as a triangle, meaning to combine or close. The square below represents a mouth or opening. The combination suggests sealing an opening, like a lid on a teapot. *Ki* means mind, spirit, or energy. The top four strokes represent the wavy lines of steam, to which was added the eight-stemmed cross representing four rice grains on a stalk. This combination originally represented the steam rising from cooked rice. The last character *Dô* means road, path, or way of life. The top portion represents hair on top of a human head. The lower left portion once meant legs walking along a path. The combination came to mean a person walking down a road; in a broader sense, a way of life.

By this original meaning, Aikidô is neither self-defense nor sport; though some schools practice and teach it as such. *Shin Shin Tôitsu Aikidô* (心身統一合氣道) meaning "Aikidô with Mind and Body Coordinated," was developed by Master Kôichi Tôhei, to distinguish from these other forms. It is the art of learning how to maintain mind and body unity in movement; correcting the self and learning to lead others according to universal principles of Ki. It is a method of training a person to keep One Point, relax completely, keep weight underside, and extend Ki under any circumstance; an advanced form of Ki development training.

Unlike some martial arts, Aikidô requires no particular advantage in size, strength, or speed in order to perform well. Because it seems to make use of the opponent's force, and appears to be strictly defensive, it has a certain moral appeal. It is usually practiced with a single unarmed opponent, but can be applied against multiple attackers, or someone bearing a weapon. The attacker approaches with an intent to grab, choke, strike, or grapple; but instead finds that he has suddenly been thrown to the ground, or reduced to immobility by a joint lock. If the attack was made with a weapon, the weapon will have been taken away.

Because the original direction and force of the attack are magnified instead of resisted, the attacker is quite literally taken by surprise; led rather than forced into submission. Any attempt to use force, or rely on some trick of speed or timing will collide with the attacker's movement, and end in a mere wrestling match. When performed well, that is with mind and body coordinated, there is great beauty and composure in Aikidô movements, for both attacker and attacked. In a typical Aikidô throw, the attacker comes in to punch (Fig. 6-2), and is led about-face in a circle (Figs. 6-3, 4, and 5); then thrown back in the direction from which he came (Figs. 6-6, 7, 8, and 9). The thrower stays at the center of the movement, and is not thrown off balance by the centrifugal pull of the opponent's body (Fig. 6-10). Being calm and centered is important throughout the throw, but essential before and after it.

Aikidô is not magic, but it is not mere physics either. Though it seems to have something in common with self-defense, sport, or even dance, Aikidô poses problems which can only be solved by mind and body coordination. Many of the skills, tricks, and attitudes which help in fighting, competing, or performing can actually hinder one's performance in Aikidô, particularly if the attacker has mind and body unified. If the attacker cooperates and takes a predetermined fall, it is easy to stage an impressive Aikidô demonstration. However real training begins when the student learns to maintain mind and body coordination under the stress of rapid movement and coordinated attack.

合氣道

Fig. 6-1

Fig. 6-2   Fig. 6-3

Fig. 6-4   Fig. 6-5

Fig. 6-6

Fig. 6-7

Fig. 6-8

Fig. 6-9

Fig. 6-10

Preserving Space under Pressure

Just as in calligraphy, there is a kind of *Ki-u* or space involved in Aikidô arts. It begins with *ma-ai* (間合), a distance at which your opponent cannot attack you without making a major body movement (Fig. 6–11). This is usually just beyond arm's reach, but a person with strong Ki can maintain *ma-ai* at any physical distance. *Ma-ai* is a distance which creates no anxiety or feeling of physical threat. In *ma-ai* one can take in the other person's whole body by peripheral vision. Maintaining this safe distance under attack is one purpose of Aikidô techniques.

Aikidô is usually practiced by two partners, *uke* is the attacker, who breaks *ma-ai* while maintaining a state of mind and body coordination. *Nage* must lead the Ki of *uke*, throwing or controlling his body without losing his own mind and body unity. *Nage* protects himself with a throw; *uke* protects himself by breaking the fall with *ukemi* (受け身), that is by falling with mind and body unified (Figs. 6–12, 13, and 14). Without proper *ukemi* the fall can be quite dangerous. Without Ki the throw is ineffective. In this way Aikidô practice helps both partners to perfect their understanding of Ki.

There is only one way to perceive and maintain *ma-ai*, and that is to keep One Point. If the mind is calm and alert, then it can apprehend the precise moment

Fig. 6-11   Fig. 6-12

Fig. 6-13   Fig. 6-14

that *ma-ai* is broken. If the body is relaxed, then it can act without hesitation to preserve the safe distance. Stand in a unified posture and ask your partner to slowly approach you until you feel that invisible line, beyond which *ma-ai* will be broken. Birds and other wild animals have an instinctive feeling for this distance, and will not let anyone get beyond it. From this distance you can see any sudden movement your partner might make, almost before it happens. Because the mind leads the body, his Ki must precede the physical movement. In a unified posture your mind is like the surface of a calm lake, able to register the slightest breath of Ki which blows across it. When you feel the movement of your partner's Ki, say "Now!" to signal your ability to respond in time. With practice, it will be almost impossible for anyone to take you by surprise. However, knowing how to respond is a matter of learning Aikidô techniques. Merely having a sense of rhythm is no guarantee of being able to play a musical instrument.

Most martial arts have a fighting or ready stance, known as *kamae*. Aikidô has none. A fighting stance is the posture of a fighting mind; one which has lost the principles of mind and body unity. Standing crouched and tense, with fists or hands ready to strike may look strong, but cannot pass any Ki test (Fig. 6-15). It may be strong against a test from one particular direction, or against one particular attack. This is why it is often used in sports, where behavior is strictly limited by the rules of the game. But *kamae* is unstable against a test from an unexpected direction, and therefore useless in a real fight. The typical standing posture used in Aikidô is known as *hanmi*, a variation on the standing unified posture in which one foot is placed in front of the other at right angles (Fig. 6-16). This narrows the portion of the body exposed to attack, and permits rapid movement in any direction. *Hanmi* is relaxed and comfortable; *kamae* is tense and braced for an attack.

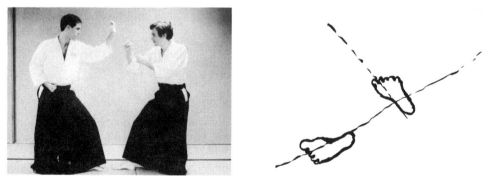

Fig. 6-15   Fig. 6-16

The tension and rigidity of *kamae* is also apparent in the eyes. When gripped by anger or fear, the range of peripheral vision becomes narrowly focused on a point. In extreme cases it may shut out everything but the opponent's face or weapon. Tension puts blinders on a person. As Aikidô training removes excess tension from the body, it gradually opens the eyes. It is not necessary to stare at something to see it clearly. You can only hit a tennis ball if you don't look right at it. Reading one word at a time slows you down tremendously. We perceive things better when we see them as a whole, rather than piecemeal.

Part of preserving space under pressure is being able to see clearly in all directions, even though you are attacked or thrown. Beginners tend to shut or narrow their eyes while they perform a technique. This is evidence that Ki has been cut. With correct practice, the eyes begin to take in everything that is presented to them, including many things that we ordinarily overlook. As the body develops more resilience and overcomes the pain and discomfort of early training, the eyes blink less frequently, and notice more. In a crowded practice room this helps avoid collisions. Open eyes acts as sentries, to alert you to any invasion of *ma-ai*, even before it happens.

It takes only a second for a person to raise a knife and cut you on a diagonal sweep. If you are slow to notice the invasion of *ma-ai*, then you will not have time protect yourself (Fig. 6-17). However if you are standing in a unified posture you can feel the intent to attack just before the knife is raised, and enter swiftly enough to throw the opponent to the ground (Figs. 6-18, 19). *Nage* enters as *uke*'s arm swings up, not after. This divides *uke*'s upper and lower body motion into two opposite directions, backward and forward, causing a loss of balance. If *nage* begins to move after he notices the movement of *uke*'s arm, he will collide with its forward swing head-on, resulting in a contest of strength.

Fig. 6-17   Fig. 6-18

It is possible to maintain *ma-ai* even with close physical contact. If *uke* grabs *nage* in a bear hug from behind, there seems to be no physical distance between them. Furthermore, *uke* is out of the range of vision. Still *nage* can throw, if he can maintain mind and body coordination. Struggling to get away, *nage* only closes up the available space (Fig. 6-20). If *uke* is strong he can squeeze the breath out of *nage*, or pull him down to the ground. However if *nage* can maintain the unified posture without raising weight upperside or losing One Point, then *uke* feels helpless to control him, as if he were trying to crush a basketball with his bare hands (Fig. 6-21). This resilience, already seen in various of the Ki tests, enables *nage* to fling his opponent off of his back by a small rotation of the hips as he steps

Fig. 6-19   Fig. 6-20

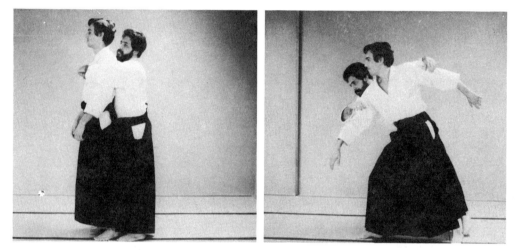

Fig. 6-21   Fig. 6-22

forward (Figs. 6-22, 23). If *nage* attempts this without keeping the One Point, he too will be thrown off balance, or will be unable to shake *uke* loose.

An Aikidô attack is like a Ki test performed with the whole body instead of just the arm. Furthermore, *uke* has mind and body unified, making the test almost impossible to pass without moving. *Nage* cannot move aside or evade *uke*'s unified attack indefinitely, so it becomes necessary to resolve it with a throw or immobilization technique. If the technique is performed without mind and body coordination it becomes reduced to a contest of strength, which the unified attacker will win. Both *nage* and *uke* must preserve space under pressure, that is maintain mind and body coordination under attack. Otherwise the practice has no significance as Ki development.

Fig. 6-23   Fig. 6-24

Unity of Calm and Action

A rapidly spinning top appears perfectly still. Violent winds whip around the peaceful center of a hurricane. In the same way, when we rapidly focus and calm the mind at the One Point, we are capable of generating energy well beyond our normal everyday capacity. Most people are caught in relative thinking: alternating periods of activity with periods of rest; never really get the most out of either. Moving without mind and body coordinated causes an excessive amount of stress and fatigue. This soon becomes evident in Aikidô practice. After an hour or more of continuous practice, the body naturally becomes tired. Those who can keep the mind fresh and vigorous easily find their second wind, and continue without difficulty. However, those who yield to the desire to take a break often allow their minds to grow tired. Without strong Ki extension they find it even more difficult to continue. In old Japan, people trained relentlessly for hours at a time in the martial arts. Very little explanation was given; only commands to continue. The result was that those who had natural ability endured and became great martial artists. Those who did not, dropped out.

Though the body obviously has physical limitations, these are far beyond what we usually assume. Cases of miraculous survival in a crisis or superhuman strength in an emergency are not unknown. As a martial art, Aikidô takes daily life with a certain seriousness; yet one which is at the same time light and positive, because it is based on the principles of mind and body unity. If we could live our daily lives with this seriousness, we would be able to live in harmony and great strength.

The essence of the unity of calm and action is rhythm. Aikidô has its own rhythm, different from that of music or mechanical motion. It begins and ends with a living calmness—full of potential energy. It is the rhythm of a good story: something occurs which builds suspense; there is a turn of events, and a conclusion which ties it together. Aikidô techniques begin without *kamae*; but they don't begin without suspense. Even before the attacker makes contact, the pressure of his breaking *ma-ai* is palpable. Like air, Ki is invisible but resists compression. The stronger the Ki extension, the greater this feeling of Ki compression. It is hard to attack someone who is strongly extending Ki; just as it is hard to look at the sun or swim upstream.

A person with weak Ki extension is an easy target for a punch (Fig. 6-24). However it is impossible to punch a person without first breaking *ma-ai*. Any punch which is strong enough to be a threat will be preceded by a strong surge of Ki. *Nage*'s response must be quick, like the sound which issues from clapping hands; but it is possible to duck under the punch in such a way that *uke* is totally taken off balance (Fig. 6-25). In this case the head is outside of the range of the opponent's knees, so that even if *uke* collides with *nage*, he will trip over the most stable part of *nage*'s body (Fig. 6-26). Obviously if *nage* jumps the gun, he will be even worse off than before. There is no advantage in trying to second-guess the opponent. Being too early is no better than being too late. Proper timing is a function of keeping One Point and moving with mind and body unified.

Fig. 6-25   Fig. 6-26

Whether or not *nage* has the proper rhythm is revealed in his foot movements. If *nage* is properly centered, the feet are calm at the beginning and at the end of the throw. The fighting mind, on the other hand, is restless; giving rise to the boxer's feet. Unified foot movements are swift and purposeful, with no unnecessary steps. Because mind and body coordination are never lost throughout the movement, *nage* moves efficiently. Even after a dozen throws in rapid sequence, *nage*'s breathing remains calm and smooth, without any special effort. *Uke* is working many times harder; being thrown to the ground and getting up again as many as twelve times in less than a minute, covering the space of a large room. Even so, if *uke* remains unified, and doesn't fight the natural rhythm of the fall, then his breathing too will calm down in a moment or two. Beginners don't know how to move, and so take many unnecessary steps; ending up breathless after a rapid sequence of throws or falls. This is not as much a matter of physical conditioning as it is mind and body coordination.

If *uke* punches at close range, there may be no time to duck under it. In this case *nage* may hop back (Fig. 6-27), leading *uke*'s fist down and up behind his back as he lunges forward (Figs. 6-28, 29), then throwing *uke* forward, projecting the arm like a spear (Figs. 6-30, 31). Like most Aikidô throws, this one is ineffective if the timing is off. The timing depends on maintaining *ma-ai* throughout the movement. *Ma-ai* may change according to the size of the opponent and degree of commitment in the attack, but the adjustment is made unconsciously. Vehicles on the road are of all different sizes, but a good driver can maneuver without collision. But even if *nage* manages to throw *uke*, he should finish the throw without losing his balance, like a bird alighting suddenly on a branch.

This is harder to do if *uke* is holding on to *nage*'s body or clothing. If *uke* grabs both of *nage*'s wrists with both of his hands, *nage* can throw him forward using a movement similar to the boat rowing Ki exercise described in Figs. 2-14 through 2-19. Stepping back from the One Point pulls *uke* off balance. *Nage* takes *uke*'s far forward wrist with his rear hand, leading it up and down to throw *uke* forward (Figs. 6-32, 33, 34, 35, and 36). If *nage* loses One Point in the midst of all of this movement, *uke* can easily hold on to the wrists and pull *nage* off balance on the other side, with the authority of his full body weight in motion. The One Point anchors *nage*'s body, allowing it to make full use of centrifugal force; making it impossible for *uke* to hold on.

Fig. 6-27   Fig. 6-28

Many Aikidô techniques make use of a rhythmic vertical motion, similar to the Ki test for the Arm-Swinging Exercise described in Figs. 2-20 through 2-29. If *uke* attacks with a vertical blow to the head, *nage* can jump in to his side, both arms raised (Fig. 6-37), and literally get behind his attack, helping it down from above (Fig. 6-38), and leading it back (Fig. 6-39). By magnifying rather than blocking *uke*'s forward motion, *nage* makes full use of centrifugal force. *Uke*'s feet swing forward, but his upper body remains behind, held back by *nage*'s hands (Fig. 6-40), resulting in a fall (Fig. 6-41). The rhythm of this throw takes some years to learn.

Fig. 6-29

Fig. 6-30

Fig. 6-31

Fig. 6-32

Fig. 6-33

Fig. 6-34

116

Fig. 6-35

Fig. 6-36

Fig. 6-37

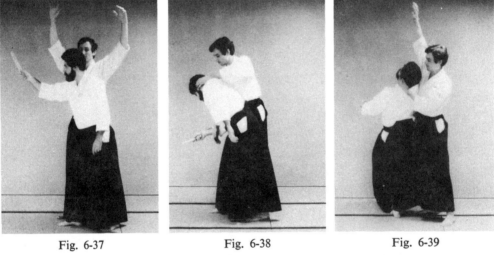

Fig. 6-38

Fig. 6-39

Fig. 6-40

Fig. 6-41

Fig. 6-42

Fig. 6-43

Because *uke* is at such close quarters, it poses special dangers if he is wielding a knife. If *nage*'s One Point is even a little too high, he will be cut by *uke*'s knife as he falls (Fig. 6-42). Practice with a wooden knife helps develop sensitivity to the proper *ma-ai* and rhythm needed to throw *uke* without being cut. If *nage* is extending strong Ki before *uke* attacks, then *uke*'s movement will be unconsiously diverted to the outside at a subtle angle. As a result, *uke*'s body will move around the center of *nage*'s One Point. But if *nage*'s One Point is too high, his own feet will be unconsciously diverted to the outside, putting *uke*'s One Point at the center (Fig. 6-43).

The closer the center of the movement is to *nage*'s One Point, the more dynamic the movement of *uke*'s whole body, and the less control *uke* has over the knife. The closer the center of the movement is to *uke*'s One Point, the more stable and controlled *uke* becomes. The problem for *nage* is to remain calm, and move in a swift but centered manner the moment *ma-ai* is broken.

The Principle of Non-Dissension

There is no dispute in the absolute Universe. Conflict is born of relative thinking. Central to the martial art of Aikidô is the principle of non-dissension. The word *budô* (武道) in Japanese means martial art; but its etymology suggests a different meaning. *Dô* means "way," as in Aikidô. The character for *bu* in *budô* is composed of two parts: one representing a spear, and the other meaning to stop, or cease using. Many martial arts today, including Aikidô, are practiced for self-defense, or as competitive sport. Being a true *budô* in the original sense of the word, Aikidô is neither sport nor self-defense. The real purpose of Aikidô is not to win out over an opponent, but to perfect and develop yourself by gradually correcting all of your movements in accordance with the principles of the Universe. When practiced correctly, that is with mind and body unified, Aikidô is Ki training par excellence.

Before learning how to lead others, it is necessary to first learn how to control yourself. Relative strength is quite limited; only a tiny portion of the strength that is available to us through Ki. One can only lead others by acting without dispute; which is not to avoid conflict, but to be totally beyond it.

Sports are played according to rules, for the enjoyment of competition. In a game, any play which violates the rules can be retaken. There is usually no danger of loss of life. In principle, a wrong decision in *budô* can mean life or death. In true *budô* there are no rules. This does not mean that it is alright to practice with real weapons, or fight to the finish. Rather it means to live life seriously, and face it with your full strength.

The essence of non-dissension is transcending technique; going beyond the opposition of *nage* and *uke*. Force can always oppose force; but it cannot oppose relaxation. A person who is unified in motion, and at rest, is stronger than one who has a fighting mind. As long as you think of adapting your movements to your partner, your thinking will be relative and your reactions slow against a unified attack. You are not likely to meet a unified attack on the street, because mind and body unification is beyond the comprehension of a criminal mind. A unified attack is used in training for mutual development. Aikidô is the way to union with Ki, or the Universe, not with *uke*'s attack.

As with Japanese characters in calligraphy, techniques in Aikidô begin with structure, and are gradually refined into dynamic movements. The problem is how to abbreviate a technique without losing power. When we learn a new skill, we often approach it step by step. Yet when we actually perform it, it is usually necessary to perform all of the steps simultaneously. Any movement, no matter how smooth, can be broken down and described by a series of steps, like the frames in a movie film. Yet step by step, most movements are impossibly awkward, or too slow to be practical. Like the frames of a film, the steps must flow together, in the proper sequence, at a speed which is beyond our perception to analyze. The movement must be edited and abbreviated without losing the story line. A good Aikidô movement is economical, containing all of the original steps within it.

It sometimes seems to the untrained eye, that an Aikidô master is throwing someone without doing anything. In fact, he or she is making a highly abbreviated, but complete movement. Beginner's are powerless to throw just by imitating this simple movement, because they move without Ki. The steps must be practiced in sequence before they can be performed simultaneously. Against a unified attack, the throw cannot be forced by being aggressive or moving quickly. It is possible to stage a throw to make it appear that the person was thrown with Ki. But like a counterfeit bill, the differences are apparent to a trained eye.

None of these techniques should be performed without the supervision of a trained instructor. Throwing and falling without the proper knowledge can cause serious injury. The following throw is presented in detail as an illustration of how an Aikidô technique is abbreviated, not as a set of how-to instructions.

Ryôtemochi Kokyû Nage Irimi: This technique involves throwing an opponent back on the ground, after he grabs hold and tries to control one arm with both of his hands.

In its fundamental form, the basic throw may be practiced in as many as seven steps. Each step is clearly articulated, like the strokes in *kaisho*, or printed calligraphy. Many Aikidô movements are unfamiliar enough that it takes some time for a beginner to learn where to put the feet, and when. This is important because there is a reason for each step, and for the sequence in which they fall. Leaving out any one of the steps can render the throw ineffective. However, even if all of the steps are mechanically performed correctly, the technique will not work unless mind and body remain unified throughout. Ki tests can be performed at any step to correct the posture. In step one, *uke* takes hold of *nage*'s forearm with both

Fig. 6-44   Fig. 6-45

Fig. 6-46   Fig. 6-47

hands, standing slightly to the outside to avoid a punch from *nage*'s free hand (Fig. 6-44). If *uke* holds with Ki, that is with a relaxed but firm grip, *nage* will find it very difficult to free the arm by force or leverage alone. In step two *nage* withdraws his forward foot, without moving the wrist at all (Fig. 6-45). Weight is then transferred to the forward foot for step three, where the rear knee is raised high off the ground, still without moving the held wrist (Fig. 6-46). In step four, the raised foot is set down near the original position of the forward foot, while bending the elbow to allow the wrist to remain in its held position (Fig. 6-47). In step five, *nage* stands up abruptly, once again extending the held arm to its original position. *Nage*'s body has still not approached *uke*, and the wrist has not been moved from its held position, so all of these movements can be made freely without opposition by *uke* (Fig. 6-48). However, *nage*'s vertical movement has created a powerful Ki extension, and moved *uke*'s mind. Now it is possible to move the held wrist freely, where it would not budge before. In step six, the arm is extended up and across *uke*'s chest (Fig. 6-49). In step seven, *nage* steps through without any resistance (Fig. 6-50), causing *uke* to fall back to the ground (Fig. 6-51). After moving the opponent's mind, it becomes easy to move his body.

As simple as it looks, it takes years to master these seven steps. Making the vertical movement without approaching or colliding with the opponent is what moves his mind. If this movement is made without mind and body unified, then the wrist tends to move up and down with the body. Any approach that *nage* makes before step six will collide with *uke*'s strength, and fail to move his mind. This may work against an opponent holding with strength, but not against a unified *uke* holding with Ki.

Fig. 6-48

Fig. 6-49

Fig. 6-50

Fig. 6-51

The first stage of abbreviation is similar to *gyôsho*, or semi-cursive calligraphy. In this stage, steps two, three, and four are reduced to a single step; making five steps instead of seven (Fig. 6-52). Step one is the same. In the next step, the position of the feet are switched by jumping, or rather dropping down into the bent-knee/bent-elbow position (step four of *kaisho*). Then *nage* stands up (step five), extends the arm (step six), and steps through (step seven). This abbreviation must be made with strong Ki, or the technique will not be effective.

The second stage of abbreviation is like *sôsho*, or cursive calligraphy. In this stage, step one is the same; steps two through six of *kaisho* are condensed into a single rapid movement, switching the feet and moving the arm like a whip; ending in the last step through (Fig. 6-53). This cannot be done unless *nage* is extending strong Ki. Abbreviating the technique this far without moving *uke*'s mind results in nothing. To a person whose mind is not focused at the One Point, it is impossible to generate any power from such a small movement. But if done properly, the whip-like motion of *nage*'s arm is almost impossible to resist.

This technique can be refined even further, to a fully cursive version that is illegible to the untrained eye. Yet even in this highly abbreviated version, all of the steps are present in the proper sequence. In the third stage of abbreviation, all of the steps are performed simultaneously, taking less than a second from beginning to end (Fig. 6-54). It has an explosive quality, caused by a powerful extension of Ki. Neither *uke*, nor any observer present may be fully aware of what happened. A whip can lash more rapidly than the eye can follow. Similarly, *nage* must be totally relaxed to whip the arm fast enough to perform the technique at this speed. *Sôsho* style Aikidô arts are most effectively applied at the moment that *uke* grabs, not after he gets hold.

There are several reasons why people tend to lose power when they abbreviate a technique. The biggest problem is trying to force the abbreviated technique to work, before having mastered all of the steps in the more structured version. Another problem is trying to move the body without first moving the mind. Unless mind and body are coordinated before, during, and after every step, the technique

Fig. 6-52   Fig. 6-53   Fig. 6-54

will not work against a unified attack. As in calligraphy, there are subtle lines and directions that can only be discovered by practice: that is by correct repetition with feedback. The secret to abbreviating the techniques without losing power is the same as the secret of maintaining mind and body coordination in movement:

Do the thing in your mind quickly,
and relax completely knowing that it is done.

Principles of Shin Shin Tôitsu Aikidô

If *uke* attacks without mind and body unified, that is with upper body tension and inherent instability; then it is relatively easy to throw his body. What happens will be governed by the physical dynamics: strength, speed, and leverage. Aikidô can be, and often is taught this way. But this defeats the purpose of Ki development. There are five principles used in *Shin Shin Tôitsu Aikidô* which help students to practice Aikidô as Ki development.

1. Ki is Extending: This is similar to the last principle of mind and body unification: Extend Ki. However it suggests that there is no preparation involved. Ki extension is a given; without which practice has no meaning. This is easy to forget when learning complicated body movements. Even for experienced Aikidô students, the tendency is to take a mental and physical *kamae* before performing the technique. Forgetting that extending Ki is a mental principle, many people extend their limbs instead. *Uke* sometimes tests *nage*, instead of attacking him; because without mind and body unity in the beginning, the throw cannot be expected to go well.

2. Know Your Opponent's Intention: If *uke* is holding with strength, it is relatively easy to throw him, with or without Ki. But if he is holding with Ki, his grip will be firm and penetrating, exerting control over *nage*'s whole body. It is impossible to lead this strong Ki without being sensitive to its direction. In order to throw the opponent, you have to know what he wants; that is, exactly how he intends to control you. When *nage* relaxes completely, then *uke*'s intentions naturally become clear.

3. Respect and Cooperate With the Direction of Your Opponent's Ki: If *uke* is applying a unified attack, it will be difficult, if not impossible to throw him by strength or leverage alone. As evident from the various Ki tests, a unified mind and body is very strong and stable. To respect that Ki means to not test or oppose *uke* throughout the throw. Because *uke* is moving, and the Aikidô techniques themselves involve a great deal of motion, it is very difficult to avoid colliding with *uke* someplace. The only way to avoid collision is for *nage* himself to move in a state of mind and body coordination. Respecting Ki also means remembering the purpose of Aikidô training: mutual Ki development.

4. Gain Cooperation by Putting Yourself in Your Opponent's Place: Many Aikidô
techniques involve *nage* displacing *uke* by occupying his position at the center of
the movement. This cannot be done except by very rapid and centered movement,
the fruit of understanding the opponent's intentions. It can never be done by
trying to force your own intentions on the opponent. That only intensifies the
spirit of opposition. *Nage* must anticipate *uke*'s intent, and be there before him to
help him fulfill it. *Uke* helps to train *nage* by making it a challenge to do this.

5. *Lead with Confidence:*   If *nage* has extended Ki, known and respected *uke*'s
intent, and physically placed himself at the center of the movement, then he will
be in a perfect position to lead *uke* without any resistance. Once *uke*'s Ki is led,
there is little he can do to prevent the throw from being completed. The only
thing he can do is control his fall and protect himself. Once in position, *nage*
should execute the technique without hesitation. If turning in a circle, then everything should turn together. Looking back over the shoulder will only kill the
rhythm of the movement by cutting Ki.

Aikidô and Ki Development

It is difficult to appreciate how powerful Aikidô throws can be without experienc-
ing them directly. However it is dangerous to experiment with Aikidô without
first learning *ukemi*. Still there are some simple Ki tests that anyone can safely
perform, which suggest something of the power of mind and body coordination.

Ask your partner to make a tight fist, and determine to keep that fist from being moved. Check his determination by pushing with your palm directly on his
fist, from above, from below, and to each side (Fig. 6-55). As in an arm wrestling
contest, if your strength is evenly matched, it should be difficult to overcome his
resistance and move his fist. However, if you can first move his mind, it is easy
to move his fist. To move his mind; with a relaxed arm, lightly hold his fist from
above, using only the tip of the middle finger and thumb (Fig. 6-56). No matter
how many times that you do this exercise, if you pause a moment before trying
to move his hand, you will feel a slight tension enter his arm as he braces to resist.
This draws his weight upperside, and makes his fist very easy to move. The more
he resists, the more rigid his arm becomes. As long as your touch remains light, he
is powerless to prevent his fist from being moved in any direction you like.

Using Ki it is also possible to bend the wrist of a person with a very strong
forearm. Ask your partner to make a fist as before, and to resist as much as he
likes; but to ask you to stop, the moment he feels any pain. Bending the wrist all
the way causes the person to fall. But if he is afraid, or unable to fall, then he
may needlessly injure his wrist by refusing to yield when his wrist has already been
bent. Measured by the thumb at the top of the fist, the fist can be rotated to the
outside (clockwise for the right hand) only 90 degrees without bending the wrist
(Fig. 6-57); and only 180 degrees if the wrist is bent, as long as the body remains

Fig. 6-55

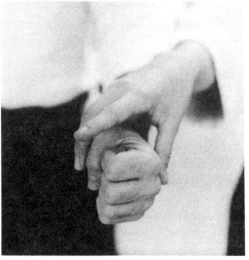

Fig. 6-56

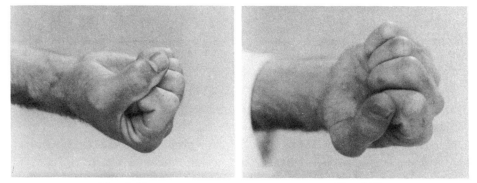

Fig. 6-57

Fig. 6-58

Fig. 6-59

Fig. 6-60

upright (Fig. 6-58). If the fist is turned any more than 180 degrees to the outside, it acts like a door knob and turns the whole body over, or injures the wrist. To demonstrate the power of Ki, it is not necessary to bend the wrist any more than the comfortable range of 180 degrees.

Stand at your partner's side facing the same direction. After he extends the fist closest to you, test his determination to keep the wrist straight by placing your close hand palm down on top of his fist, and your thumb against the back of his hand. Cover the outside of his fist with your other hand, and try to twist his fist at the wrist, with the objective of making his knuckles point to his face (Fig. 6-59). As long as you are using strength he should be able to easily resist your force and keep his knuckles pointing forward. Because the mind leads the body, it is necessary to lead his Ki before trying to bend his wrist. The fingertips act like a nozzle for the Ki extending out of the arm. If you can control the direction of the fingertips, you can easily bend the wrist and control the whole arm and body. Hold his fist as before, but touch it very softly. Using the fingertips of your outside hand, press his fingertips into the center of his palm. This creates an inward spiral of Ki, following the line of his fingertips; making the wrist very easy to bend (Fig. 6-60).

If the wrist can be moved or bent despite any amount of muscular resistance, then it is possible to apply any number of Aikidô throws and joint-locks. It is relatively easy to do these exercises standing still; but another matter to do them in the midst of dynamic movement under a unified attack. But the principle is the same: first unify your own mind and body, then you can easily lead and direct others.

Ask your partner to take firm hold of your right wrist with his right hand. If you try to use force to lift or pull your wrist away, you directly collide with his strength (Fig. 6-61). However, if you simply reach up and scratch your head with your right fingertips, either your hand will suddenly pull free, or he will be power-

Fig. 6-61   Fig. 6-62

less to stop you (Fig. 6-62). It requires no effort to do this. We do it hundreds of times a day without thinking about it. He is holding your wrist. But your finger-tips, which are the nozzle of Ki, are free to move in any direction. It is not a question of which is stronger; there is no comparison.

If your partner holds both of your wrists apart with both of his hands, and tries to prevent you from touching them together, you will have trouble overcoming his resistance with force (Fig. 6-63). But you can easily move your hands if you clap them together and applaud him in front of his face (Fig. 6-64). Enthusiastic applause is filled with Ki. The body is much stronger when the mind is positive. It is very difficult to restrain a person who is extending Ki.

Fig. 6-63   Fig. 6-64

Sometimes it is necessary to overcome the force of not strength, but weight and inertia. Both you and your partner take opposite ends of a towel in the right hand, letting it hang loosely between you (Fig. 6-65). Ask your partner to brace himself in a stable position. Then you suddenly pull hard on the towel, trying to pull him off balance or make him move his feet (Fig. 6-66). As in a tug-of-war, it should be very difficult to overcome his resistance with force in kind. If you gently take up the slack in the towel before you pull, then you move his mind, and make his body easier to move (Fig. 6-67). Taking up the slack baits the hook and moti-vates him to move in spite of himself. It may appear that the *uke* in an Aikidô demonstration is cooperating and taking the fall. Actually it is *nage* who is coope-rating with and baiting *uke*'s intent to attack. It is not necessary to wait for *uke* to decide what to do. *Nage* can help determine what *uke* will do by offering an invitation to *uke*'s Ki. That invitation is sometimes difficult to turn down, in spite of efforts to resist. The reason for this is that once *uke*'s mind moves, he has al-ready taken the bait. *Uke*'s resistance is ineffective, because it is too late. His mind is already going in that direction, and he cannot help but follow. The only way *uke* can regain control is to go along willingly, without losing mind and body unity. This is *ukemi*. If *uke*'s mind-body unity remains unbroken, then *nage* will have difficulty throwing him, unless he too can deepen his own state of mind-body coordination. In this way both *uke* and *nage* develop stronger Ki.

There is a certain strength in stubborness, but it too can be overcome with Ki. Ask *uke* to stand firm; determined to keep his head upright. Gently place your four fingertips on the side of his head, at the temple, and try to push his head to the side (Fig. 6-68). His neck is likely to be stronger than your fingers, so he can probably resist without much effort. To move his head, you must first move his Ki. There is a tendency to consciously push on the surface or side of the head that you are touching. This puts tension in your arm and fails to move his mind. With a totally relaxed arm, touch the side of the head with the fingertips again; only this time, consciously push on the other side of his head, as if your fingers were long enough to penetrate that far (Fig. 6-69). It is painful to resist, so most people move their head out of the way without hesitation. Because mind and body are one, once the mind has been moved it is very difficult for the body not to follow. Forcing the body to remain behind is painful.

None of these Ki exercises are Aikidô techniques in and of themselves, but they do suggest the power that lies in an Aikidô throw. *Uke* is often thrown a distance several times his own height, making it necessary to take *ukemi* with mind and body coordinated to avoid injury.

Fig. 6-65

Fig. 6-66   Fig. 6-67

Fig. 6-68   Fig. 6-69

Implications for Daily Life

Even civilized Man is a territorial animal. The need for space results in competition and often ends in violence. Aikidô develops a sensitivity to personal space, through *ma-ai*. But it also gradually changes one's entire attitude toward space. The One Point is the center of the Universe, but it is not a fixed point. Nor is it a personal possession. The One Point is something we all share, and deserves mutual respect.

Unlike something which can be made personal property, the One Point cannot be protected with a fighting mind. Aikidô teaches us that the only way to really find personal space is to help others to do the same. Aikidô cannot be performed or learned alone. It requires another person. Competitive contests are not permitted. Students in *Shin Shin Tôitsu Aikidô* are ranked on their ability to demonstrate mind and body coordination in movement. In the higher ranks, the techniques become increasingly difficult: disarming an opponent, dealing with multiple attackers, and performing a precise sequence of Aikidô arts within a specified time limit. The ability to do all of these things comes from a deepening of the student's comprehension of Ki. Without this, there is no meaning in simply learning how to throw people.

It is impossible to successfully perform Aikidô in a negative frame of mind; it doesn't work. Regular practice of Aikidô gradually changes the subconscious mind, teaching it to respond positively to problems and challenges. It is a practical working philosophy for dealing with any crisis. For most people, it takes years of practice to throw off the longer years of negative thinking which have preceded it. Training is hard, but not training is also a form of training, in reverse. As long as we live, we practice something. The important thing is to develop good habits of movement in our daily activities.

7. KIATSU: *KI and Massage Therapy*

Difference between *Kiatsu* and *Shiatsu*

Shiatsu (指圧) is a form of therapeutic massage making use of finger pressure. *Kiatsu* (氣圧) appears to be similar to *shiatsu*, but is based on entirely different principles, making use of Ki pressure. *Kiatsu* was also developed by Master Kôichi Tôhei; in an effort to teach people how to use Ki to heal themselves and maintain health. There are several different forms of *shiatsu*, but most of them make use of physical force and body weight. *Shiatsu* and other forms of massage often knead the tissues with the ball of the fingers, the heel of the hand, or even the knees and elbows. In *Kiatsu*, only the fingertips and hands are used, to take up the slack and extend Ki directly into the tissues.

If overdone, *shiatsu* can injure the patient. Excessive physical force breaks up the stiffness and resistance temporarily, but the next day the patient's muscles are often stiffer than before. Repeating this kind of rough treatment makes the muscles so stiff that the *shiatsu* therapist has to work harder and harder to achieve the same result. The therapist himself may become so tense in this, that he too loses mind and body coordination and may even become sick as a result of giving treatments. These are known as the shoulders which killed the masseur.

Ki is a limitless energy, freely available from the universe to anyone who knows how to receive it. As long as the *Kiatsu* therapist knows how to coordinate mind and body, there is no danger in giving *Kiatsu* treatment. However it should not be given carelessly, because incorrect technique creates tension, and can have the reverse effect.

How to Press with Ki

The fingertips are used in *Kiatsu* because they act like a nozzle to focus and concentrate Ki. Tension turns this Ki inward and restricts its flow. A relaxed arm curves naturally at the elbow. If the arm and fingers are held straight and stiff, then the arm can easily be bent by a partner of equal strength. Ask your partner to place the palm of his closest hand on top of your elbow, and try to bend your arm from below your hand, using the leverage of your forearm (Fig. 7-1). Though

| Fig. 7-1 | Fig. 7-2 | Fig. 7-3 |

you resist with the strength of your arm, equal strength will succumb to leverage. Next shake your wrists vigorously from the One Point, and let them come to a calm stop. Raise the arm as it is, without straightening the elbow or stretching the fingers (Fig. 7-2). Though the arm is relaxed, your partner will find it many times harder to bend, if he can do so at all (Fig. 7-3). The arm may feel firm while it is being bent, but this is different from the tension arising from active resistance. If you tense your muscles, you will fail. If your partner tenses your muscles, you will be strong. You are responsible for what you do, not for what your partner does. Equal strength is no match. Leverage can be effectively applied to a rigid object.

The feeling in the arm is similar to that of a firm handshake. Awareness is mostly in and beyond the hand itself. If you become too conscious of his hands at your elbow and wrist, then you will gradually receive and succumb to his bending force. No matter how hard he tries to bend, your arm remains totally relaxed because you don't receive his Ki. If he breaks *ma-ai* by approaching you as he bends, just keep the proper distance by allowing your feet to move when he approaches. If he applies more force at the wrist than at the elbow, your arm may come up, but there is no reason for it to bend. You can prevent this by keeping weight underside. The arm muscles may become full under the stress of his bending action, but this taut feeling should disappear the moment he lets go. He put the tension there; you merely absorbed it. The purpose of this exercise is to extend Ki, not the arm. When done properly, your partner will even lose the desire to try to bend your arm the moment he touches it.

The unbendable arm is a natural function of Ki. But the arms were made to bend at the wrist and elbow. Otherwise we would be unable to use them. The arm is relaxed, so it can be extended and withdrawn freely, even under pressure. While your partner continues to try to bend your arm, you may move it up, down, in and out as you like (Figs. 7-4, 5). He can only stop you if you cut your Ki by re-

Fig. 7-4   Fig. 7-5

sisting his motion directly. When giving *Kiatsu* the arms must have this kind of power.

Kiatsu is given with the fingers, not the arms; so the fingers also must be unbendable. Stiff fingers spread wide apart are extremely weak. Extending Ki is a principle of the mind, not the body. The fingers are strongest when slightly bent, like the arm. The middle finger is slightly longer than the others, so the four fingertips can be lined up straight when pressing on a flat surface (Fig. 7-6). In this position the fingers act like a jet nozzle on the end of the unbendable arm, concentrating and accelerating the Ki extension. These fingers are strong enough to move a large person aside. Ask your partner to stand stubbornly in your path. Walking from the One Point, approach him and extend the unbendable arm and fingers to his chest and keep walking (Fig. 7-7). Because you are breaking *ma-ai* in a kind of unified attack, he must move aside. If his feet are slow to move, he may feel a momentary sharp pain where your fingers touch. Be sure to get One Point before you extend your arm. Otherwise you will lose mind and body unity when you raise the arm, and it will bend on his chest. Against a large person, an arm without Ki is no better than a paper sword.

It is not enough to simply extend Ki from the fingers to give *Kiatsu*. There are no totally flat surfaces on the body, so Ki must be directed at very precise angles to reach the injured tissue. The first step in doing this is to keep your conscious attention at the fingertips when giving *Kiatsu*. Without considerable training, it wanders away to other things the moment we lose mind and body coordination. When Ki is extended into an object through the fingertips, the fingers seem to take root in the spot. Spread your fingers slightly and touch the wall with all five fingers, thumb toward the floor. Mentally extend Ki "roots" into the wall, and ask your partner to try to slide your hand in any direction along the wall, while holding your wrist (Fig. 7-8). Though you make no special effort beyond this, your fingertips won't budge. If you forcefully resist this motion, tension will pull up

132

Fig. 7-6

Fig. 7-7

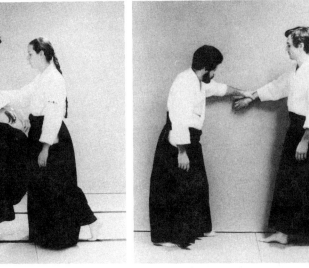

Fig. 7-8

Fig. 7-9

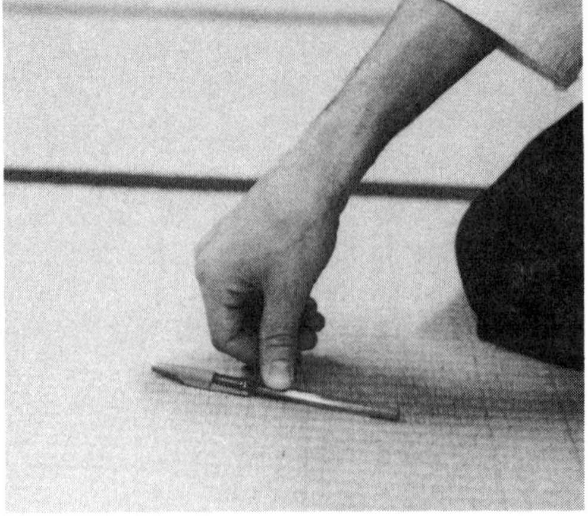

Fig. 7-10

the roots and your hand will easily slide along the flat surface. Pushing your fingers hard against the wall merely pushes them away from it. Pushing your fingers into stiff muscle tissue creates an even greater rebound. In self-protection, stiff muscles will prevent you from getting to the root of the problem.

Weak tissue recoils from strong stimulation. The muscles surrounding the weak area close over it to form a kind of body armor. Most bodily tissue is pliable and resilient. There are many directions in which the tissue can recoil and escape. The diseased tissue must be coaxed out into the open, so that it can receive full exposure to the incoming Ki. Because this is mostly a reflexive response, it is not usually under the conscious control of the patient himself. Therefore the *Kiatsu* therapist must learn to direct the Ki at very precise and subtle angles. This process can be simulated by using the thumb to pin a pencil or pen to a flat surface. If the ball of the thumb is used, as in some forms of *shiatsu* (Fig. 7-9), then the pen can easily be flicked or pulled out from under. In this case, Ki flow is not only restricted by tension, but its direction out of the fingertip by-passes the pen altogether. Because the tissue can escape so easily, the treatment is often ineffective, or takes longer. If the tip of the thumb is used to press perpendicularly to the surface, directly into the pen, then the pen cannot be easily knocked or pulled out from under the thumb (Fig. 7-10). This is only a rough simulation of *Kiatsu* treatment, because bodily tissues are much softer and more pliable.

According to Ki principles, the mind and body are one, and cannot be divided into parts. Likewise Ki must not be directed to a single part alone. Good *Kiatsu* pins the patient's whole body to the spot. When Ki finds root in a spot which needs it; not only the desire, but the very ability to escape, temporarily leaves the patient. Ask your partner to sit with good posture in a straight-backed chair. Standing behind him, you can test his posture by pulling back lightly on his shoulders with your fingertips, palms down. If he is stable, he will have One Point and be in the strongest position to stand up. But he will be unable to do so if you pin his shoulders from above with Ki. Place each hand between his neck and shoulder on both sides. Extend Ki into the shoulder from the front with the fingertips, and from the upper back with the thumb (Fig. 7-11). Though there is no more weight on his shoulders than that of your hands, he will find it nearly impossible to stand up from the chair. This gives the patient a very pleasant and protected feeling. It helps him to relax, and draws the injured tissues to the surface for treatment.

Disease makes the patient more aware than usual of some part of his body, either through pain, dullness, or fatigue. This disrupts mind and body harmony, and makes the muscles tense. When mind and body are coordinated, you are not conscious of your muscles or physical weight. *Kiatsu* helps return the patient to health by restoring mind and body unity. Though the *Kiatsu* therapist may touch two different parts of a limb, when bathed in Ki the two parts feel like one. Hold your partner's wrist and forearm palm up from below, with both hands. Find two spots on the top of the forearm with the tips of each thumb (Fig. 7-12). If you squeeze the arm with strength, he will easily be able to feel both spots, even with eyes closed. To hold his arm with Ki, gently take up the slack on each point, extending strong Ki from the tip of each thumb. Now the two spots should feel like

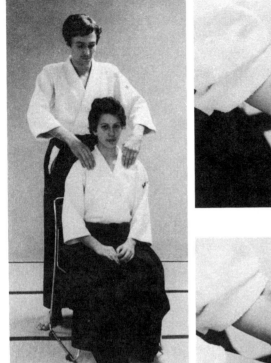

Fig. 7-11

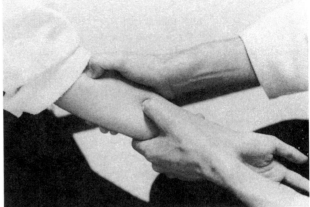

Fig. 7-12

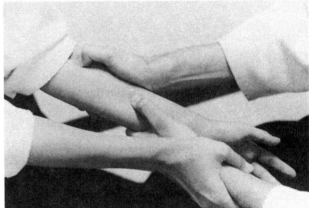

Fig. 7-13

one, even with eyes open. This feeling is very pleasant, and the patient may lose any desire to pull his arm away. He may be surprised to find that he can't, even if he tries. A similar principle was once used by Chinese policemen, using a tightly woven tube made of straw. Inserting a finger from each hand into the tube was easy, but the tube tightened its grip whenever the criminal tried to pull his fingers out; making them a very effective form of handcuffs. Even if he uses the other hand to push on your forearm, it will be very difficult to pull his arm free (Fig. 7-13). This ability cannot be abused, because it is impossible to injure the patient holding his arm in this way.

Though modern medicine knows how to repair injuries and make artificial organs, it cannot make Ki, the life force itself. Though a great deal is known about Pathology, the world is far from free of disease. No one can truly grasp what creates life and heals disease. The mechanisms of Physiology are rather well known, but no one knows what starts it and keeps it going for so many years in perfect balance. Ki principles do not offer modern medicine any new information, but they do put it into a fresh perspective. They show the relationship between good posture, mind and body coordination, and good health.

Why Things Go Wrong with the Body ―――――――――――――――

Good posture is any body position in which mind and body are unified, especially in movement. It is the only thing which ensures a steady exchange of Ki with the universe. Poor posture puts pressure on the nerves which radiate from the spine; the peripheral nervous system, which regulates most of the involuntary processes that maintain life and health. This pressure disturbs the vital network of communication within the body, eventually resulting in disease or injury. Good posture itself is regulated by Ki, which we can increase by Ki development.

Stiff muscles reflect the body's attempt to hold together the untidy package of an uncoordinated body. Movement aggravates the stress, creating wear and tear, just as in an automobile with poor wheel alignment. If the lapses in mind and body unity are few, then muscle stiffness will be infrequent or limited in scope. Some peoples' minds and bodies lead separate lives; held together only by the bands of tension which crisscross the body.

Stiff muscles tear easily—especially under the shock of violent movement in sports. The typical response of modern sports medicine is to tape and immobilize muscle and tendon injuries. But muscles fibers are elastic, and shrink when they are immobilized. Isolated under a cast, they will slowly grow back together, but healing and rehabilitation take months. Even a serious tendon or muscle injury can be fixed in a matter of days or weeks; minutes if the injury is treated immediately after it occurs. Many injuries only begin at the moment of the shock, when the Ki suddenly recoils from the area of impact. If the Ki can be coaxed back right away, the injury will be light, or may not even occur. Continuing to move an injured muscle without mind and body coordination subjects it to a series of random shocks, to which it is powerless to respond. This is why doctors immobilize the area. Careful rehabilitation is necessary along with *Kiatsu*, in order to coax the life force back into the area, and reeducate the muscle. Even a partially torn muscle can be strong and unbendable if the mind and body are unified. Taping or putting a cast on the area allows the muscles to atrophy. The injury actually gets worse before it gets better. Sometimes the tissues that tear are well below the skin. It is impossible to get access to these places without being able to rotate and move the limb. Still for serious injuries, an amateur should not attempt to perform *Kiatsu* therapy. To do so without proper training and supervision is almost certain to make things worse.

Ki development training prevents most common injuries, because it increases the body's ability to absorb stress of all kinds. However, it is still necessary to stretch the body every day to maintain good posture. To this end there are five simple stretches, known as *Makkô-Hô* (真向法), which can help maintain good posture.

They take only a few minutes to perform, but lose their effectiveness if they are not done once or twice a day, every day. Even if the body were to gain or lose a single millimeter of flexibility each day, over time will it amount to a big difference.

All of the *Makkô-Hô* exercises are performed on the floor, on a firm but comfortable surface. For people who have grown up away from the floor, sitting in soft chairs and sleeping on soft beds, these stretches may be difficult in the beginning. Children can perform them without effort. In nature, stiff branches break; branches which are young and flexible bend easily. Use *Makkô-Hô* as a barometer of your youth, more accurate than your chronological age. The only reason to become discouraged is if you stop doing them. Because both progress and deterioration are progressive, perseverance is more important than how flexible you may be at the moment.

For the first stretch, sit on the floor with your legs extended out to the front (Fig. 7-14). Try to push the back of the knees flush to the floor with the palms of the hands. This is important, to position the lower back for the stretches that follow. Stretch the back of the knees further by pushing the heels out. Throughout this stretch try to point the toes to the face. Bend the upper body forward, trying to touch the floor beyond your toes without bending the knees (Fig. 7-15). This is done in two sets of five repetitions.

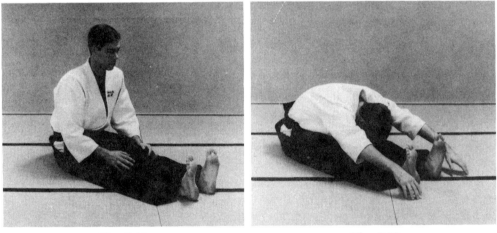

Fig. 7-14   Fig. 7-15

For the second stretch, spread the legs as far apart as possible, keeping them straight (Fig. 7-16). Take hold of the left foot with the left hand, and try to touch your head to your knees (Fig. 7-17). After five rhythmic stretches on the left side, lift the foot with the hand and open the left leg a little further. Repeat the same thing on the right leg, and then again on both sides, each time opening the legs a little more. This stretches the legs and lower back at different angles than the first exercise.

Go right into the third exercise from that position, bending forward to try to touch the chest to the floor (Fig. 7-18). This stretches the inside of the legs.

Draw the legs in for the fourth stretch, holding the balls of the feet face together with both hands (Fig. 7-19). Try to stretch the inner thighs first by tapping

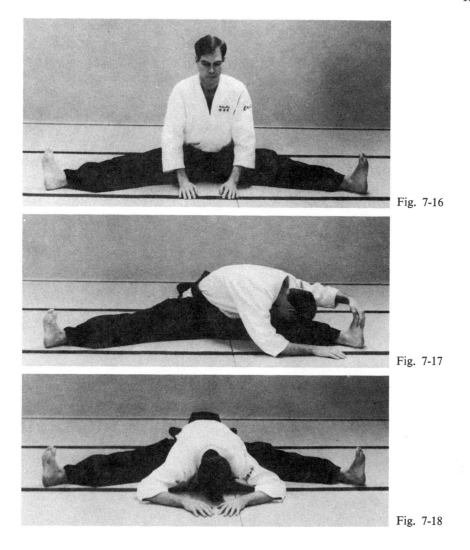

Fig. 7-16

Fig. 7-17

Fig. 7-18

the floor on both sides at the same time with the knees (Fig. 7-20). Then stretch the base of the spine by bending forward until the head touches the floor (Fig. 7-21).

The fifth and final stretch begins in *seiza*. Lie back, and fold your hands together, invert them, and stretch you palms to the outside, away from your head (Fig. 7-22). Try to keep the knees on the floor. Turn the upper body from side to complete the stretch.

It takes years of daily practice for most adults to perform these *Makkô-Hô* stretches as fully as described here. Any angle which is closer to the ideal is a significant improvement, because lack of practice carries you steadily away from the goal. Years of habitually sitting with the "tail" tucked under, rather than out behind, gradually make the entire body stiff. The legs and pelvic region become so stiff, that it may be hard to sit in a unified posture, even in a chair. This deformation can not be corrected overnight. But it is a dangerous handicap, which will take its toll on your health in time, if it is not at least partially corrected.

Fig. 7-19   Fig. 7-20   Fig. 7-21

Fig. 7-22

Fig. 7-23

There is no need to panic if you are very stiff; steady daily practice is sufficient. However, if you want to become more flexible in a shorter period of time, you can enlist the help of a partner. As long as the body is not forced to take more than it can handle, your partner can assist you by pushing or leaning on your back (Fig. 7-23). Remembering that the partner's help is only a supplement, use it with discretion.

If the legs and hips are very stiff, then the knees may not lay straight at all. When the knees are forced to touch the floor, the body may not bend any more than 90 degrees at the waist. This is not unusual in the beginning, particularly for those who lead a sedentary life. However, this is where the stretch begins: at the knees and the pelvis. The stretch is almost worthless if it doesn't include these two places, which are posturally related. Keep the back as straight as possible when you stretch. There is no advantage to bending the upper back just to be able to touch the floor with the hands.

Muscle stiffness can be treated by giving *Kiatsu* directly to the stiff areas. Muscle stiffness usually spreads across the body in complex patterns. A drawing of the muscle anatomy only shows a static picture (Fig. 7-24). Rotating or stretching the limbs reveals entirely new surfaces.

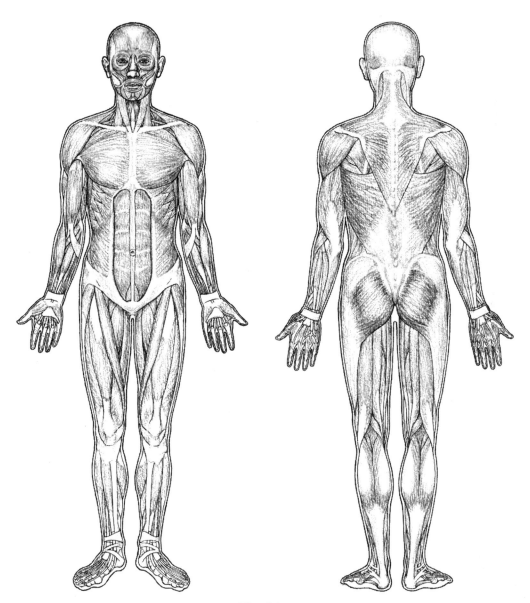

Fig. 7-24

Lack of mind and body coordination also weakens the abdominal and other organs. Most organic functions are involuntary. They operate more or less independently of our conscious control. The stomach, intestines, liver, kidney, and other organs go unnoticed until something goes wrong. Through stress, abuse, or fatigue, the organ stops functioning smoothly; throwing our daily life out of rhythm. Each organ has a rhythm and a tone all its own, normally regulated by the autonomic nervous system, as long as poor posture doesn't interfere. When weight is poorly distributed in the body, it does more than just strain muscles and nerves; it restricts circulation and breathing, further cutting the supply of Ki to the vital organs.

Modern medicine typically responds to alimentary, metabolic, and endocrine problems with drugs. In serious cases, doctors don't hesitate to use surgery, or even to replace the defective parts with artificial ones that don't wear out. No miracle of biomedical or chemical engineering can ever restore the life force once it has faded. Drugs may keep people alive, but they don't strengthen the body or develop Ki. Take the drug away, and the person is weaker than before. If you must take drugs for a health problem, don't second-guess your physician by prescribing your own doses. Practice Ki breathing for at least an hour a day, and rebuild your strength with Ki development. As Ki restores life and vigor to your organs, they will gradually lose their dependence on the drug, and you will be able to do without it in time. If the problem is not serious, don't bother to take drugs in the first place.

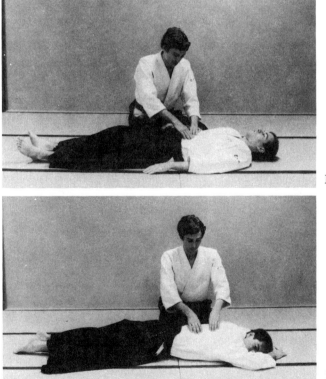

Fig. 7-25

Fig. 7-26

Kiatsu may be given directly to an ailing organ; most of which are accessible on the abdomen (Fig. 7-25), or on the back (Fig. 7-26). Before an organ breaks down or contracts a disease, it usually loses its natural tone; becoming swollen or flaccid. An experienced *Kiatsu* therapist can quickly detect an organ that has an abnormal tone. *Kiatsu* can help restore the organ to its normal tone and functioning.

Nervous problems like insomnia, neuroses, neuralgia, and headaches; circulatory disorders like high blood pressure and arteriosclerosis; and respiratory difficulties including colds and allergies; are all closely related to problems with mind-body unification. Irritability and anger bring the weight upperside. Attitudes of both fight and flight contribute to blood pressure and put stress on the heart. Stress can even trigger allergic responses and skin rashes. All of these problems respond best to regular Ki breathing, Ki development exercise, and *Kiatsu* treatment on and around specific problem areas.

Principles and Concepts of *Kiatsu*

By way of summary, the use of Ki in *Kiatsu* therapy can be explained in five basic principles. Most of these have been explained in this or previous chapters, so they will simply be listed here for reference.

1. *Extend Ki from the One Point.*
2. *Do not Let Tension Accumulate in Your Body.*
3. *Press Perpendicularly toward the Center of the Tissue without Damaging it.*
4. *Concentrate on the Infinitely Small Movement of Ki at the Fingertips.*
5. *Work on the Lines instead of the Points.*

Simple lines are taught in the *Kiatsu* curriculum. They follow the natural contour of the anatomy. These lines are not related to or derived from the meridians and points of acupuncture and *shiatsu*; which are based on ancient and often archaic Chinese cosmology and astrology. These lines were no doubt once based on similar insights. But like many old religions, over the centuries acupuncture has become overburdened with layers of theories and interpretations. Like the flat earth theory, some of these are based on assumptions which are scientifically untenable. They may serve as a useful starting point for acupuncture researchers, but they should not be accepted simply because they have endured for centuries. Healing is more of an art than a science. Much depends on the attitude and life force of the patient himself. Focus should be on the patient's health; not on how well he conforms to ancient theories. We live in the same universe as the ancients did. There is no reason why we can't learn directly from it, rather than from them.

In clinical *Kiatsu* practice, lines do appear. Within the limits set by human anatomy, they tend to be unique to the person and the conditions of the illness. They are as individual as fingerprints; and it takes a skilled therapist to find and treat them accordingly. When one line or angle appears to have recovered, another one seems to surface, that neither patient nor therapist were conscious of before. Once the patient's own Ki flow has been restored, it is more effective to continue the treatment by teaching Ki development. All of the basic disciplines which develop Ki require a certain basic level of health, from which they take the process deeper.

Sometimes *Kiatsu* is painful; in the same way that exercise and physical training can be painful. Assuming the therapist is not violating any of the basic principles, this pain is a sign that new barriers of resistance are giving way. As the area relaxes, new lines and angles surface, and the pain gives way to more pleasant sensations. If the problem is small, the area may be ticklish, rather than painful. As healing takes place, the patient's body can take more and more pressure, until any line feels good under pressure. *Kiatsu* is a special kind of Ki test, applied directly to the injured or diseased areas, to test their resistance. As long as the tissue is alive, it will feel something. If it feels nothing, it may be dead, or partially paralyzed.

In *Kiatsu*, pressure is applied just until the slack is taken up. Any more than this causes a different kind of pain; an attack, not a therapy. Strong Ki may be able to repel it, but there is a line which separates, and joins Aikidô and *Kiatsu*. Healing takes place most rapidly when the pressure is maintained just at or beyond this borderline. As healing takes place, this line recedes and disappears, until no area is painful or tender under an equal amount of pressure. The process is similar to the healing of a scar, but takes place in a very short period of time.

The Japanese word for sickness is *byôki* (病氣), or ailing, troubled Ki. The word for health is *genki* (元氣), the origin or source of Ki. *Kiatsu* restores the patient to health by calling forth the patient's own life force, right from the source. Before a dry pump can draw well water, it must be primed. *Kiatsu* helps prime the patient's own wellsprings of Ki. Ultimately it is the patient who heals himself by restoring mind and body unity.

Shiatsu therapists sometimes become weak from the tension and fatigue that hard massage produces. Inexperienced *Kiatsu* therapists must also be careful, for they are subject to the same problem if they lose mind and body coordination. If the therapist treats many patients, and works too much on the body, without also correcting the negative states of mind which accompany sickness, then he too can get sick. Negative attitudes are far more contagious than microbes. Their effect is immediate, but often unconscious. Doctors sometimes die of their own specialty. They live and breathe a certain disease year in and year out. It takes strong Ki to be able to avoid being affected by the fear which surrounds that disease.

Illness can come from the mind as well as the body. Every time we utter a single negative, angry or fearful word, we lose mind and body coordination in that instant. This can be verified by testing a person the moment after he makes a pessimistic remark, and comparing that to what happens when he states any of the Ki principles with understanding. Positive words call forth Ki; negative words hold it back. Notice the topics of conversation of people who are healthy and energetic, and compare them to those of hypochondriacs and complainers. As they talk about their past and present circumstances, they unconsciously frame their futures.

A *Kiatsu* therapist needs strong Ki to help his or her patients become more positive. Without practicing Ki breathing for at least an hour a day, it is inadvisable to give too much *Kiatsu* to other people. Unless you know how to replenish your own supply of Ki, your patients may draw it out faster than it comes in. A person who extends Ki out without relaxing completely to receive a fresh supply, may even faint on the spot.

Implications for Eastern and Western Medicine

It is commonly assumed that Eastern medicine, especially acupuncture and *shiatsu*, are more natural in their approach to healing than conventional Western medicine. Yet both Eastern and Western medicine are similar in their symptomatic approach to disease. Western medicine uses more extreme forms of intervention; drugs, surgery, and high-technology. But Eastern medicine is often equally obsessed with stimulation, albeit of meridians and acupuncture points. The references to Ki (*Chi*, or *Qi*) in acupuncture theory are often too abstract and contradictory to be of practical use. So modern acupuncturists look for measurable changes in the body; though they may follow ancient prescriptions and theory.

Ki works too fast and too mysteriously to measure and tie down. But we can direct it with our mind, and achieve tangible results. It enters freely into a broad heart and an open mind, and blesses it with good health.

8. The Strategic Game of GO

How Go is Played

In his novel, *The Master of Go* (Published by Charles E. Tuttle Co., Inc., 1972), Yasunari Kawabata describes the ancient Oriental game of *Go* as a game of abundant spiritual powers, encompassing the principles of the universe and human life. The game was invented perhaps 4,000 years ago in Tibet or China. It has survived and thrived. Today it has tens of millions of followers, all over the world. Its technique and philosophy have been most fully developed in Japan, where eight million amateurs and over 400 professionals now play the game.

Go is played on a 41 1/2 cm by 44 1/2 cm (16 3/4″ × 19″) board, marked by 19 vertical and 19 horizontal lines. On the intersections of these lines are placed white or black lens shaped "stones," in order of each player's turn (Fig. 8–1). Each stone earns its right to remain on the board as long as it can "breathe" through one of the life lines extending from the point on which it rests, to an open breathing point adjacent to it. It may also breathe vertically or horizontally through any adjacent stone of the same color (Fig. 8-2). In order to accomplish this, players take turns staking out territory; attempting to surround, and therefore capture and eliminate enemy stones.

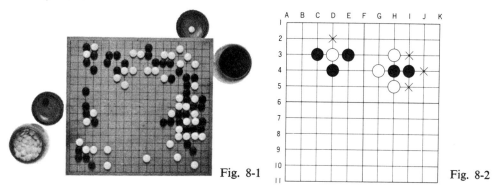

Fig. 8-1   Fig. 8-2

The territory is large, but limited; like an island. Any empty space with a breathing point adjacent to it at the end of the move is fair game. The possibilities for strategic development are endless. Territorial points are counted at the end of the game, in terms of the number of points which your stones surround.

Groups of stones are vulnerable to attack until they are secured, by controlling two independent breathing spaces, or "eyes" within the group. A point is also earned for each captured piece. There are so many possibilities and unpredictable relationships between groups of stones, that it is impossible to cover every one by logical anticipation. Only by seeing the whole picture, with all of its potential, can the player make moves which have the greatest possible impact and meaning. Thoughtless and reflexive moves lead quickly to defeat. A short game can be finished within thirty minutes. More typically, games last an hour, to an hour and a half. Professional games can involve twenty to thirty hours of play.

A good *Go* player is quiet and irrepressible; challenging the opponent by flushing out his weaknesses without respite. But aggressiveness alone is self-defeating. Without a calm mind, the player dangerously overlooks his own weaknesses.

Go develops a tolerance for ambiguity and incompleteness. Beginners tend to see only the trees, and overlook the forest. Many petty exchanges are like traps. Early victories are seductive and deceptive, because they can narrow the player's view of the whole board. The game requires intense concentration; but tension upsets the mind and limits perception of potential. *Go* teaches a person to concentrate on a complex and changing situation, under intense competitive pressure; while remaining relaxed enough to make good judgments. It has historically been viewed as a superb game of war strategy.

Going beyond Thinking You have Understood ─────────────

The moment you think you have understood a problem, your mind begins to grow old. You may have grasped part of the problem, but most problems in *Go* are more complex, or simpler than they appear. This is not only true of *Go*. A simple example of this is the phenomenon known in *Go* as "false eyes" (Fig. 8-3). In this diagram, black appears to have three eyes, divided between two different areas. For a group of stones to be invulnerable to invasion, it must have two safe, non-adjacent eyes. Black's three stones in the lower right are threatened with capture at point F-3. This would leave only two adjacent points in black's territory. Either one could be filled in by white in a subsequent move. If black were to take the invading stone, that would leave only a single eye remaining; which white could fill in the next move, and take the entire group of black's stones. Black gains nothing by connecting his two groups of stones at point F-3, because the end result is the same.

Though a group like this is already lost, a beginner may waste precious moves trying to save it. In the early game, the potential for later loss or benefit is so great, that wasted moves cannot be afforded. Thinking that you understand a situation is dangerous, because it causes premature and thoughtless decisions. Investing in a situation that has no hope is bad, but missing out on other opportunities is worse.

This is analogous to responding to a Ki test by tensing the body and directly resisting the hand that tests you, rather than making the body stable and unified as a whole. A unified group can repel any attack. But if a group lacks internal strength, it crumbles under pressure.

Shun the Profit and Loss at Hand, for the Sake of the Whole ───────

There is a strategic concept in *Go* known as "thickness"; which refers to a loose concentration of stones, not yet a solid group, but possessing inherent strength. Players attempt to build thickness on their own side, and stay away from it in enemy stones. Thickness is reserve power: a readiness to respond, expressed in the strategic location of the stones. Corners are strategically important in building thickness (Fig. 8-4). Here white's group is strong, both inside and out. It offers no weak points for black to invade. The corner serves as an anchor or base from which to spread to the center. Black's stones at points B-6 and C-7 are free from danger for the moment, but they serve no useful purpose. Black's stones at E-2 and E-3 are threatened with capture in one or two moves, and have no prospects for survival. White outnumbers black only ten to eight, but the loose placement of white's stones gives them a power many times that ratio. In this case, black is advised to play away from white's thickness, and begin to build some of his own. One way to do this is to play at M-3, loosely near his existing stone at P-4. This gives black the same potential two-stone lead in the right-hand corner that white enjoys in the left.

Loose concentrations are stronger than tight ones. Internal space is what gives strength to a character in calligraphy as well. Mind and body unification is realized in the same way; with a relaxed body and strong Ki extension. Creating this internal space is a matter of training and intuitive perception. It cannot be reasoned or calculated into existence. Nor can it be created by imitating form alone. Thickness is the result of mind and body unification; a visible expression of an invisible strength.

Thickness is shunning the profit or loss at hand, for the sake of building strength in the whole. Relative strength is temporary, and only effective on a small scale. It is caught up in the immediate pressures of the moment. When the mind is calm, it ceases to act in haste, and develops an enduring strength. This is reflected on the *Go* board by the development of thickness.

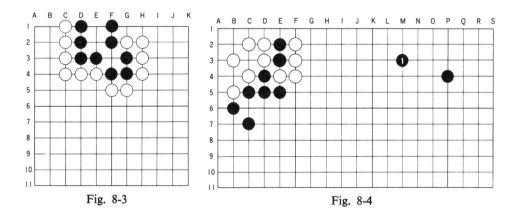

Fig. 8-3   Fig. 8-4

Patterns Discovered—Patterns Remembered ———————————

Jôseki (定石) or "fixed stones" are established patterns of corner play. As master patterns of good play, they make very good study material. Like a straight jacket, *jôseki* problems seem to offer no escape. Yet a subtle solution to the problem does exist, and it is up to the student to find it. Some people make great efforts to memorize *jôseki*, so that they can be used in an actual game if a similar situation arises. The problem is, that the same situation never arises twice. Treating a new situation strictly in terms of a similar but unrelated pattern merely dulls the mind. Memorized *jôseki* lead to errors in perception and judgment. *Jôseki* are best forgotten once they have been learned.

Corners are some of the most prized territory on the *Go* board. Once secure, they are easy to defend, because fewer stones are needed to protect the group. This increases the relative power of any stone placed in the region of a corner. They also provide a base for connecting with other groups of stones later in the game. Unified and connected groups upset the stability of all opposing groups of stones nearby.

Jôseki illustrate how a group of stones can be won or lost, sometimes in only one to three moves. They are like close races, where a single wrong step can determine the outcome. Like puzzles, the primary benefit is found in trying to solve them for yourself. It is impossible to look up the answer in a real game. Few problems in life come with a set of instructions. Books designed to teach *Go* techniques list problems and answers on separate pages, so that the reader can try to solve the problem for himself. Computers and hand-held calculators are available which offer a chance to play out *jôseki* until the right answer is discovered.

Jôseki are difficult to visualize without having the benefit of a playing board and pieces. Some attempt can be made by drawing circles and dots on graph paper. Several *jôseki* are presented here for reference, showing sequences of effectve play (Figs. 8-5, 6, and 7).

In the *jôseki* in Fig. 8-5, black is almost entirely surrounded by white; yet black manages to take control of the corner by playing at B-1, a strategic point. White responds at G-1, taking black's stone at F-1; but without securing a lifeline for his own group of stones. Black's next move at C-2 makes it impossible for white to save his group. Furthermore, black has a strong foothold, with two independent eyes.

Fig. 8-6 illustrates another simple *jôseki*. Black starts out on the inside of white's stones at the corner; but white disputes black's claim to the territory with a threat at B-1. According to the *jôseki*, black's most appropriate response is to play the corner itself, at A-1. This stone is sacrificed to white on the next move at A-2. However, black can now have what white cannot: by playing at C-1 black entraps the two white corner stones and secures the corner.

Fig. 8-7 shows a *jôseki* that is less tight than the first two. This time black is on the outside, and the corner as yet belongs to no one. However, black can take control of the corner by playing the *jôseki* pattern at B-1. Black can now prevent

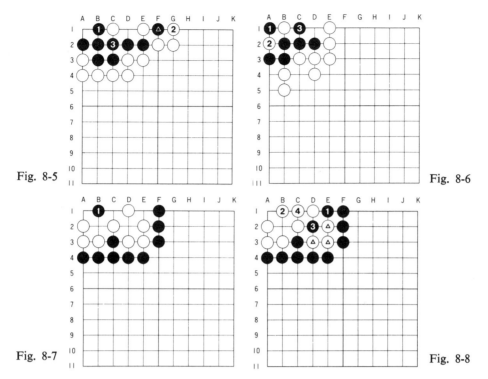

Fig. 8-5

Fig. 8-6

Fig. 8-7

Fig. 8-8

white from forming two independent eyes; all accomplished in a single economical play.

However, as shown in Fig. 8-8, suppose that black had gone after the three white stones at D-3, E-2, and E-3 instead. This could be accomplished in two moves: at E-1 and D-2. But it would only result in a few points; and it concedes the corner to white. Without stable groups, anchored in the corners and along the edges, merely capturing pieces for points has little meaning.

Jôseki make useful patterns for study of master play, but they will rarely appear just like this in a real game. Even if a familiar *jôseki* were to appear, its value would depend on the situation in the other corners and at the center of the board.

Even though a student may make many mistakes in attempting to solve a *Go* problem on his own, experience teaches better than theory. It doesn't require much Ki to memorize what to do in case of a problem. The struggle to solve our own problems calls forth an instinctive response from the life force. Ki tests are like *jôseki* for daily life. They show us the difference between true and apparent strength. It is up to us to apply what we have learned in facing personal and professional problems.

Don't Be Concerned with Winning; Just Polish Your Skill

Go is a contest. That is an unavoidable fact. Playing to win does develop relative strength. But in relative strength, everyone meets his match sometime. Not being concerned with winning does not mean treating the game lightly, as though it was only a game and the outcome didn't matter. The purpose of the game is not only to win. If winning was the only objective, then it would be easy; just limit your playing partners to weaker players. The purpose of the game of *Go* is to build spiritual strength, and refine the powers of judgment. Playing *Go* does not automatically develop these qualities; it merely provides an opportunity to do so. Likewise a calm mind and strong Ki prove invaluable in playing the game. This is particularly true in a game like *Go*; where the multiplicity of possibilities quickly overwhelms both the logical faculty and the spirit of aggression. There is more to learn from defeat than there is from success, if the mind is open. Polish your skill.

Concern with winning is based on fear of the opponent. If you overcome this fear, you win victory over yourself. This is what makes it possible for you to play at your best. Most Go players learn this the hard way, if at all; through experience. Ki training could reduce the time required to learn to play the game well.

Don't Set Premature Limits on Your Strength

As we grow older, we become set in our ways. We crystallize our image of who we are, and of what we are capable of doing. This is reinforced by both education and career, which encourage people to fit ready-made molds, and produce rather than grow. As this attitude hardens in, we gradually lose our capacity for fresh and effective action.

When we seek safety and security, we sometimes unwittingly invite danger. *Aji* (味) is a term used in Go; literally meaning "taste," but referring to the quality of lingering potential. A player whose stones have *aji*, still has options. It is important to retain *aji* as long as possible. In other words, don't burn your bridges behind you. The potential of *aji* may or may not materialize, but its influence will be felt throughout the game.

Aji-keshi (味消し) means removing the taste, or killing the potential in a group of stones. It is an unnecessary move which seals off the potential for development of a group of stones, thereby wasting its potential value later in the game. *Aji-keshi* is a very subtle concept; one that involves some knowledge of the game to fully appreciate. For reference, the development of *aji* is shown in Fig. 8-9. An illustration of *ajikeshi* is shown in Fig. 8-10. Black's play at B-2 forces white to take black's stone with D-2 in self-protection. Black's stone at D-3 was vulnerable, but contributed *aji* to the situation as long as point D-2 was open. Black's play at B-2 is *aji-keshi*. In Fig. 8-11 black allows the *aji* to remain. Even though white can take point B-2 as well, this does not force black to respond immediately. Instead it leaves black free to make a potentially valuable play elsewhere on the board, and leave the *aji* in this corner. *Aji* is similar to thickness. To retain *aji* is to leave one's options flexible and open. *Aji* is reserve power. There is no need to spend it prematurely.

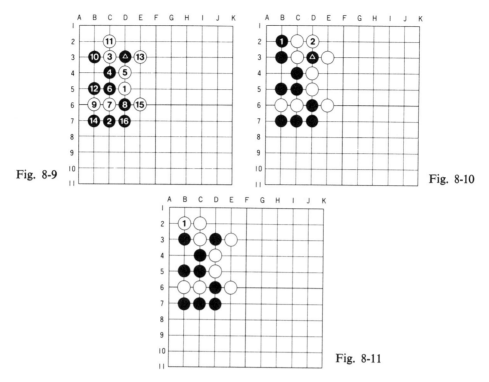

Fig. 8-9

Fig. 8-10

Fig. 8-11

There is Always a Weakness in Any Defensive Posture

A defensive shape is considered to be clumsy or heavy. It lacks internal space, and is easily crushed under attack. Good *Go* strategy involves light, open development. Given this configuration (Fig. 8-12) after white's move #4; a heavy or close black move at point D-6 would be crushed in a few move's by white's next response at point D-8. A better play for black is move #5 at E-7; making a light shape, and leaving space for the development shown in the next six moves (Fig. 8-13). The resulting development means life for black's group of stones. Black develops

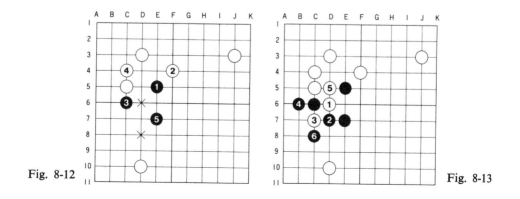

Fig. 8-12

Fig. 8-13

strength from the outside in, because of the light shape developed early on. A defensive posture may be strong in one direction, but its possibilities are very limited. The strongest posture is a natural one; internally spacious and light.

This is true in the shape of groups of stones on the *Go* board; and it is true in terms of the game as a whole. The moment you wish bad luck on your opponent, your own luck leaves you. The game can not be won by guessing, or relying on weak wishes. Real strength comes from training. The fruits of your study appear in a crisis, long after you have seemingly forgotten them. But this is only true if they have penetrated your subconscious mind and become a part of you. If you train in a state of mind and body unification, the benefits of your study will stay with you. If you play *Go* with the wrong attitude, then it will do little to develop your Ki.

Listen to Advice Like a Lamb; Take it Like a Lion

Advice can come from many sources: books, your opponent, your experience. An open mind is strong, because it can take opportunities to grow and correct itself. Too often pride and narrow vision prevent us from taking advantage of opportunities for growth. Your actual condition speaks more about you than your plans and the way you promote yourself. In this way, your performance in the game can serve as a mirror for self-development.

Weak players change their attitude according to who they are playing against. A Japanese proverb says that, "Even an inch worm has half-an-inch of spirit." This means not only that we should take care of the feelings of those weaker than ourselves, but that even a weak creature is sometimes capable of fighting with great spirit. One of the characteristics of the game of *Go*, is that its underlying ambiguity offers many attempts for reversal, even late in the game; particularly if one of the players is inattentive and makes a foolish move.

In Kawabata's novel, he describes a chance meeting he had on a train, with a foreigner who wanted to play a few games of *Go* with him. The foreigner was described as a beginner, who lost game after game. What bothered Kawabata, was the fact that his opponent seemed totally unconcerned about losing; nor did he seem to learn anything from it. He had taken lessons at the *Go* association, and had memorized some *jôseki*, but seemed to think it silly to take a game seriously.

The term *sente* (先手), literally meaning the first or upper hand, suggests a move which takes the initiative. A *sente* move forces the opponent to respond with a *gote* (後手), or defensive move which loses the initiative. It is the move with initiative which wins out. A good *Go* player will make you feel this pressure throughout the game; forcing you to respond reflexively, never getting a chance to make a move of your own choice. This is much what happens when you fail a Ki test; as you upset your basic mind and body unity in an effort to repel or defend against the incoming Ki. It is easy to pass the test if you absorb the pressure at the One Point, keeping the mind undisturbed. If you assume a superior attitude, your weaker opponent may turn on you, as the cornered rat does to its pursuer. And in the game of *Go*, this can result in a turn-about victory for the weaker player.

Go players are in constant danger of harmful oversights. The quality of irrepressibility in an opponent helps to improve one's own skill. Attitude, more than any knowledge of techniques as such, determines whether or not one has the spirit of *Go*. One bad move tends to call forth another. Losers give up mentally long before they lose on the game board.

Go: Implications for Gamesmanship

Go is practiced today on everything from hand-held computers (Fig. 8-14), to large, table-like boards (Fig. 8-15); but it is usually played on a thick, flat game board (Fig. 8-16).

There are simple rules of etiquette which are observed in the game of *Go*, which help calm the mind. By themselves, they may seem arbitrary, but in light of Ki training they have significance. *Go* players are sometimes advised to count slowly and silently to ten after realizing that they have made a foolish mistake. Perhaps this helps to settle the mind; although keeping One Point is faster. Players are advised to think of the next move without touching or fingering the stone before playing it. Leaving the hands calm in your lap allows you to see more clearly. A calm body reflects a calm mind. A calm mind and a determined spirit are the best weapons in Go; and the best allies in life.

Fig. 8-14

Fig. 8-15

Fig. 8-16

Many of the other rules of etiquette have to do with remaining calm, and showing respect for the opponent. And unless they are interpreted in this sense, they are meaningless.

- Don't watch the games being played on either side of you while you are involved in your own game. (*Note:* many games are played in the same room in *Go* clubs.)
- Don't yawn during the game. If you are that bored—do something else.
- Don't hum or make unnecessary noises.
- Don't watch the clock.
- Don't stare at your opponent's face.
- Don't drum your fingers on the board.
- Don't jiggle or play with the unused stones.
- Don't take back a play once it has been made.
- Don't watch the game while leaning on your elbows.

These rules of etiquette may appear to be no more than matters of common courtesy. However, they are not easy to maintain in a game where one move may take from five to thirty minutes to decide. Even sitting and doing nothing for that period of time is nearly impossible for most people. *Go* is filled with ambiguity. When the relentless pressure of the game gets under the skin, it is very difficult for a beginner to maintain calmness of mind. When the mind is upset, most of these bad manners appear, and the person positions himself for defeat.

However, winning is not a matter of mere bluff. *Go* is not a game of chance. In Japanese, one does not play *Go*, one "strikes *(utsu)*" it; suggesting an action much closer to the spirit of the game, than does the English word "play." The main thing, is to not run from the fight. Stay cool-headed to avoid making mistakes.

Kawabata expressed the contrasts of attitudes found in a master and an ill-mannered younger player. The master "seemed to grow larger when he seated himself before the *Go* board." He had "the power to quiet his surroundings." The young man, though carrying a professional rank, had the rude habit of keeping a magazine open on his knees during the game, and reading it during his partner's turn. "I heard one day that the young player had shortly afterwards gone insane. Perhaps, given the precarious state of his nerves, he could not tolerate those periods of deliberation."

9. *The* Noh *Drama*

A Brief Background

Noh (能) drama is one of Japan's oldest forms of theater; a masked song and dance drama with highly stylized forms, dating from the 14th century. *Noh* means ability, or skill; a character appearing in many other words suggesting potential, technique, efficiency, essence, and talent. The forms still practiced today were heavily influenced by a medieval playwright and performer named Zeami. Heavily influenced as well by Zen Buddhist philosophy, *Noh* was very early patronized by the *Shô-gun* (将軍), and by the 17th century, had many followers and amateur enthusiasts, particularly among the court and *samurai* class.

Zeami himself was very concerned with performing *Noh* so that it could reach all of the people in the audience, to pacify the spirit and promote long life. Training in the performing arts of *Noh* was and still is a matter of serious discipline and lifelong study. Traditionally beginning professional training at the age of seven, a performer's art often does not truly mature until well into middle age.

Noh shares some things in common with the Greek tragedies: making use of masks, a chorus, and often portraying other-worldly scenes with moral or religious significance. *Noh* is performed in mime, dance, poetry, and song, with colorful costumes. Properties are few in number and highly stylized.

The pace of a *Noh* play is measured and powerful. Like a dramatic and visual form of *Haiku* (俳句) poetry, extraordinary impact is achieved with great economy. The lyrics are so archaic that they cannot often be understood by modern Japanese theatergoers without specialized study, or a text in hand. Performances of *Noh* originally lasted all day, with several plays, each lasting from one to two hours, punctuated by breaks and light comic interludes called *Kyôgen* (狂言). Today, abbreviated performances of just one, two, or three plays is the norm, with one or two *Kyôgen*.

The *Noh* stage itself is designed to amplify sight and sound. It expands into the audience on two sides, from a long bridge-way by which the actors enter and exit (Fig. 9-1). This requires the actor to be highly effective in three dimensions, as he can be seen from both front and side. The floors are made of unfinished Japanese cypress wood, highly polished from use; so much so that it shows the actor's reflection. *Noh* is performed above the head level of most of the audience, under a roof which is much larger than the stage itself. The skillful juxtaposition of curved lines and overlay of roof beams visually amplify all that goes on below.

All plays are performed before a single backdrop, the *kagami-ita* (鏡板), or

Fig. 9-1

Fig. 9-2

Fig. 9-3

"mirrorboard," on which is painted a knarled and ancient pine tree (Fig. 9-2). Entrances and exits are made through a curtain, along the *hashi-gakari* (橋懸), or bridge-way, marked by three small pine trees at regular intervals as visual markers for the actors (Fig. 9-3). Traditionally, large earthenware or concrete jars were concealed at various angles beneath the floorboards, to further amplify the sound when an actor stomps his foot in performing a vigorous dance, although today, modern stages sometimes employ different means to achieve the same ends.

Because of its subtlety, its pace, its ancient Japanese roots, and its relative inaccessibility to Westerners, *Noh* is one of the more difficult of the Japanese arts to appreciate. Yet when *Noh* is performed well, it expresses Ki in a hauntingly direct way, leaving a lasting impression on the viewer's mind. Within Zeami's writings are contained many statements about *Noh* training and performance. Still considered the highest authority on the performing arts of *Noh*, Zeami's writings leave no doubt that he had a profound understanding of Ki as well.

Quotations from Zeami's Writings

"What is felt in the heart is ten; What appears in movement is seven." ──

Zeami valued what he called "Delicacy within Strength." Saying that the feeling in the heart is stronger than what appears in movement, is a classical way of suggesting that the mind leads and controls the body. Poor actors confuse acting with mere exaggeration or excitement; which on the stage, has little power to move an audience. Immature actors try hard to express what is in their minds or heart. As a result they act it out, as though it was something apart from themselves. A Japanese proverb suggests that a hawk with real power rarely displays its talons. It requires some years of training to gain enough self-mastery to restrain movement without losing power. The power, that which is felt in the heart, is Ki. The best way to restrain movement without also restraining Ki is to relax the body, but not the spirit. In *Noh* acting this is often done by focusing one's mind in the lower abdomen. Sometimes strength may also be focused in the fingertips, while relaxing the rest of the body completely. The hands are often the only part of the body visible to the audience, under the mask and massive costume. When dynamic movement is called for, the strength in the actor's hands may form a striking contrast to the sensitivity and precision required for the actor's dance (Fig. 9-4).

The use of a mask not only prevents the actor from relying on facial expressions, but many of the gestures themselves are highly stylized. Weeping is traditionally expressed by holding the palms and fingertips in front of, but apart from the forehead (Fig. 9-5). This is not merely a symbol, designed to represent sadness. The emotion emerges from the play itself, nurtured by the actor, and culminates in a gesture of great emotion, with restraint. A mature actor with strong Ki can deeply move an audience with this simple gesture. The gesture must emerge from the emotion; from the actor himself. If the gesture precedes the emotion, then the body leads the mind, and the result is nothing but a mere shell.

Fig. 9-4   Fig. 9-6

Fig. 9-5

Noh is often performed without a mask. The principal actor usually holds a simple property in one hand: a fan, a sword, or an article of cloth. If Ki is projected into the property through the fingertips, then it comes alive; an extension of the actor's body (Fig. 9-6). There is strength in the fingertips, but the arms are held relaxed, apart from the body. Though the feet are close together, there is no sense of being top-heavy. Though he is without a mask, his face is mask-like. This apparent immobility is quite different from that of a marionette. Rather it seems supported from within, projecting enough strength to command the entire stage.

Even the musicians must hold their instruments with Ki, and show a similar degree of mind and body unity. The chorus, and some of the musicians sit in the *seiza* position, often for the entire performance of a play. The relaxation is evident in the hands of the *taiko* (太鼓) drummer (Fig. 9-7). The drum sticks must be held softly enough to modulate the sound; yet firmly enough to maintain control. This relaxation extends to the entire upper body. It is very difficult to play the *taiko* for long in the *seiza* position if the weight in the arms is upperside.

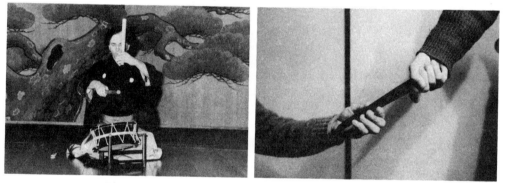

Fig. 9-7 Fig. 9-8

It is more difficult to maintain mind and body coordination when holding an object. A stick or any similar object should be held with Ki: lightly enough to allow the arm to relax completely, yet firmly enough to prevent the object from being pulled out of the fingertips. Though your partner grips the other end of the stick and pulls tightly, you can easily hold on to it with your fingertips (Fig. 9-8). It is possible to hold on to the stick by gripping it tightly; but this may cause your whole body to be pulled off balance. Any object is best controlled by Ki, not muscular strength.

"The eyes look ahead, and the spirit looks behind."

Though not obvious from the outside of the mask, the actor's vision on stage is extremely limited. A photograph of the inside of a mask shows how the actor's vision is limited to that which can be seen through small slits (Fig. 9-9). These tiny windows permit visual access to no more than a fraction of the stage at a time. If

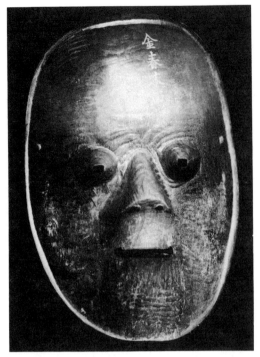

Fig. 9-9

the mask slips, the vision may be blocked altogether; with no chance to adjust the mask. Awareness of position must be achieved through sound and feeling, as well as sight. Otherwise there is the danger of backing into one of the musicians, or even falling off of the stage. Though rare, this occasionally happens in *Noh* performances.

Actors are taught, that if it feels as though one may fall off of the stage, then the actor should jump, to maintain dignity and control. The effort of trying to catch one's balance can produce the opposite effect. There is a story of one actor on the bridge-way who was supposed to set one foot on the railing during the performance. His vision was restricted by the mask, and as a result his foot missed the railing, stepping instead over the edge. Missing the railing caused him to lose his balance, which he tried to recover as he fell. However, in doing so he pulled the pine tree down with him and created a big commotion. It is difficult enough to keep balance with the eyes open. With the eyes as good as closed, it is doubly important to maintain a firm center of gravity in the One Point.

Though the eyes can only see ahead, the spirit can be aware on all sides. This awareness is apparent to the audience, not just in the fact that the actor avoids collisions, but in the actor's appearance when his back is turned. As the actor enters and exits, and performs various dance movements on the stage, his back is often turned to large numbers of the members of the audience. Yet when the actor projects strong Ki, his appearance from behind never looks small (Fig. 9-10). This has far more to do with the actor's ability than with the size of the costume. Though the actor is facing away from the audience, there is something powerful and unapproachable about his appearance.

Fig. 9-10

Fig. 9-11

The actor creates this peripheral awareness in part through his *kamae*, or basic stance and way of walking (Fig. 9-11). Lowering the hips, and holding the arms out to the side like bows, the actor glides along. The movement remains low, from the One Point. The arms do not swing, but remain in position; except when performing a stylized gesture or movement. Walking in this way, the actor appears to be pulled from every direction, and seems to glide along without friction.

The power of the *Noh kamae* is not only visual. When standing with mind and body unified, and held by a partner from behind, it is almost impossible for your partner to pull you back (Fig. 9-12). This is even easier to maintain if you assume a *Noh*-like *kamae*, with arms slightly forward and the little fingers extended outward, palms down. In this position it should be easy to walk forward, pulling your partner off balance (Fig. 9-13). However, if you are too conscious of your partner behind you, and try to force him off balance, you disturb your basic mind-body unity, and can easily be pulled back (Fig. 9-14). If done with proper Ki extension

Fig. 9-12

Fig. 9-13

Fig. 9-14

Fig. 9-15

Fig. 9-16

and relaxation, the *Noh kamae* has the power to lead the audience with deep dramatic expression.

Another Ki exercise also illustrates how projecting the awareness forward, also increases it behind. Stand in the unified posture, with your attention fully directed to the front. Ask your partner to stand behind you, extending his hand, and his mind, fully in your direction with a very positive attitude (Fig. 9-15). Ask him to maintain this position for an unspecified number of seconds, without breaking his concentration. Do this until you can comfortably focus your mind forward, and still feel his presence with you. When both of you have developed the ability to maintain this forward looking concentration, then ask your partner to silently break it by closing his fist and making an angry face at some moment. If your mind was properly directed forward, then you will be able to sense the change and spin around to signal that you have caught it (Fig. 9-16). If you are quick, you will be in time to see him close the fist. If you allow yourself to be distracted by wondering when he will close the fist, then your timing will be early or late. The secret is to be calm, and extend your mind forward. This will give you broad peripheral awareness, even behind yourself.

This experience is not uncommon among drivers who sense an approaching tailgater, before they see it in the rear view mirror. Nor is it unusual to be sitting in a large crowd, and turn around for no apparent reason, to look someone in the eyes, who has been staring at you silently for some time. Occasionally appearing accidentally in daily life, this ability is highly developed among *Noh* actors.

"Express everything by doing nothing."

The *Noh* drama is perhaps best known for its masks. Many people mistakenly assume that a *Noh* mask is neutral and expressionless. Yet the same mask can take on a subtle change of expression when seen from a different angle (Figs. 9-17, 18). The subtle transformations of a masked face reveal themselves best in slow motion, making masks most suitable for the slow, measured pace of *Noh*. Far from being expressionless, the *Noh* mask is open to endless possibilities. Far from hiding the soul of the actor, it opens a window to it.

The mask is the essence of the role, and the essence of expressing everything by doing nothing. Carved from cypress wood and painted by master craftsmen, many *Noh* masks in use today are hundreds of years old. In addition to their great artistic value, some people consider the masks to be sacred. Some actors spend many hours and days contemplating a mask before a performance. Many very old masks are cracked, stained, or warped with age; but these masks are often the most powerful on stage (Fig. 9-19). The most demanding roles in *Noh* are those with the least movement, often requiring the actor to be perfectly still for long periods of time. The *Noh* stage is like an energy field, in which the actor must command space by the power of his spirit.

The chorus, musicians, and sometimes the actors themselves go without masks.

Fig. 9-17   Fig. 9-18

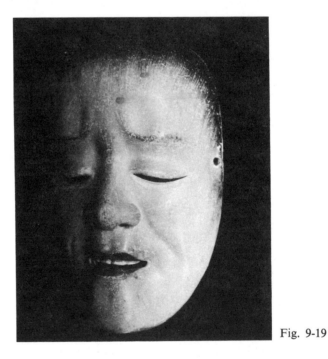

Fig. 9-19

And yet the faces are never casual or distracted. It is as if beneath the mask is another mask, the subtlety of which cannot be fathomed (Fig. 9-20). Even when none of the actors is wearing a mask, *Noh* is still a masked performance. The mask-like bare face of the main actor in this case is called *hitamen* (直面), literally meaning "direct face"; the honest face, as it really is.

All the while, the actors and musicians are required to perform skills which are

165

physically demanding and mentally rigorous. Far from doing nothing, everyone on stage must be extremely alert to what the others are doing, and where they are. Yet when the activity of the actors is too evident, the result is a very boring performance, like a meaningless ritual. The responsibility of the actors is to reveal the inner depth of the play, without making it obvious.

Part of the subtlety of *Noh* expression is the way it takes the mind in one direction, and leads it in another. Though a novice might easily miss them, there are many surprises in a *Noh* performance. For example, a *taiko* drummer may raise his right hand high, as though to strike (Fig. 9-21); only to strike with the left hand, which had been poised at a lower level above the drum (Fig. 9-22). Part of the fascination of *Noh* is not, doing nothing, but doing something slightly different than expected. This subtlety unfolds the drama and opens the mind.

Fig. 9-20

Fig. 9-21

Fig. 9-22

166

"Violent body movement, gentle foot movement; Violent foot movement, gentle body movement."

Some parts of the *Noh* dance involve raising one leg high, and stomping down (Fig. 9-23). The earthenware jars below the floor can magnify this sound like a drum. But sometimes the actor's foot strikes the floor without making a sound. This is the kind of unexpected juxtaposition of opposites which can make a *Noh* dance very dramatic and exciting to watch. Zeami often wrote of this contrast of two opposites, in one mysterious harmony. His students were advised to show the heart of a man in the form of a demon; or the figure of a strong warrior with a splintered heart. This contrast is often expressed in the difference between upper and lower body movements. Vigorous and commanding movements with a halberd, may be entirely performed sitting on a chair (Fig. 9-24).

Fig. 9-23   Fig. 9-24

"Communicate first by hearing, then by sight."

Music on the *Noh* stage is produced by four musicians and a chorus. There is no conductor. The rhythm must be created by mutual give and take, relying on signals from the drummers. No score is used during the performance; but it is not enough to merely memorize one's own part. It changes slightly from one performance to another, depending on the variations in these signals, and the flow of the performance, intentional or otherwise. The notation which is used during practice indicates the melody, and the basic rhythm (Fig. 9-25). Though the score contains instructions, what actually occurs in a performance may be different. Furthermore, no one uses the score during the performance, and there is no conductor to keep everyone to it. It must be created anew on stage.

The primary signal used by the musicians is the *kakegoe* (掛声); a cat-like yowl or percussive shout by the drummers, which tells the other musicians, the chorus, and the actors, where the group is in the play (Fig. 9-26). Though the rhythm is created by the group itself, without a leader, the timing is sometimes so precise, that a long-drawn *kakegoe* can release a drumbeat and the stomp of the dancer's foot at the same moment, though neither is watching the other.

Fig. 9-25   Fig. 9-26

Fig. 9-27

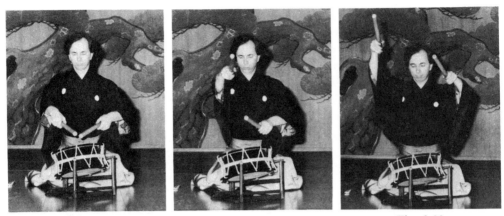

| Fig. 9-28 | Fig. 9-29 | Fig. 9-30 |

Fig. 9-31

Fig. 9-32

Two of the drummers sit on low stool-like chairs. The large, side hand-drum (*ô-tsuzumi*) (大鼓) and the small, shoulder hand-drum (*ko-tsuzumi*) (小鼓) are both struck with the fingertips (Fig. 9-27). The head of the *ô-tsuzumi* is made of a very heavy horsehide; hard enough, that hitting the drum with any tension in the hand can be very painful. For both hand-drums, the hand hits the rim of the head, and the fingers bounce off of the middle of the drum with a whip-like motion. As with the *taiko* drum, a relaxed hand produces the best sound, and affords the most control. Hitting the hand drums repeatedly with too much tension in the arm, will leave the hands swollen and sore.

The *taiko* drum can be used to draw both the ear and the eye into its hypnotic spell. A climax can be built, by alternately playing the right and left hand from higher and higher levels; beginning low and building up tension with height (Fig. 9-28, 29, and 30). In concert with the drummer's *kakegoe*, the *taiko* alone can make a captivating performance. In fact, many amateurs study only a single one of the *Noh* performing arts; and isolated parts of the *Noh* drama often draw audiences for performances. *Noh* dance, known as *mai* (舞), is very popular among amateurs. Even performed without full costume, effective use of the fan and background screens can make the audience feel the presence of invisible walls and structures. The actor's Ki leads the mind, and his artistic expression stimulates the imagination.

The *Noh* flute is also a curious instrument, with unique properties that help weave the spell of the *Noh* drama (Fig. 9-31). Inside the flute is a very thin tube or pipe, which gives it very unusual acoustical properties. This extra inner pipe upsets the normal scale in subtle ways. The lack of a scale with regular intervals, gives the *Noh* flute an otherworldly sound. This is complemented by the deep and skillfully restrained voices of the chorus, who sing and narrate the story. The performing art of the chorus is known as *utai* (謡) (Fig. 9-32), and is also popular among amateur enthusiasts.

Many actions on the *Noh* stage are preceded by words or sounds. This has the effect of leading the mind into the drama, rather than letting it simply follow the story by watching the action. This is similar perhaps, to the use of counting, to lead Ki in various Ki exercises. Sounds can have a powerful leading influence on the mind, and they are used with great sophistication in many of the Japanese arts. Centuries of refinement in closely guarded secret traditions have produced in the *Noh* drama, a form of music which may sound at first alien to Western ears; but offers us entry into a rich and beautiful expression of the spirit of Ki.

"First truly become the thing you are acting; then find the skill to imitate it."

Professional *Noh* actors traditionally begin training at the age of seven. They spend many years learning the basic skills of *mai* and *utai*, *Noh* dance and singing, before they begin to have a good sense of the specific roles of *Noh*: old person (Fig. 9-33), female (Fig. 9-34), demon (Fig. 9-35), and youth (Fig. 9-36). A young *Noh* actor must learn to transcend himself in playing roles for which he has no personal life experience. This is perhaps true of all forms of acting; but in *Noh* it has deep historical roots in Buddhism and Japanese culture. However, though men often perform women's roles, they do not change their voice, as in *Kabuki* (歌舞伎) theater. *Noh* does not strive for realism, but speaks rather to the subconscious mind, rich in symbolism and beyond time and space.

Well before appearing on the stage, the *Noh* actor is absorbed in his role (Fig. 9-37). Partly for this reason, the actor receives assistance in putting on the many layers of cloth that make up his costume. And even once this is done, the actor spends time in front of a mirror in a special room, contemplating and becoming one with his role, before he assumes the mask (Fig. 9-38). In this way the mask emerges from deep within the actor himself. Rather than being a disguise or a false face, the *Noh* mask is a window to the soul of the actor. If the actor can maintain mind and body coordination throughout the performance, the mask will amplify his spirit. If he becomes tense or confused on stage, it will be insufficient to conceal the flaws.

Fig. 9-33

Fig. 9-34

Fig. 9-35

Fig. 9-36   Fig. 9-37

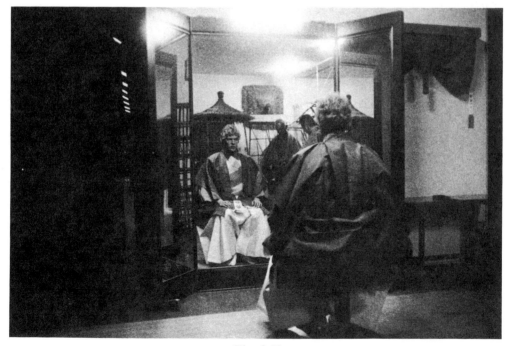

Fig. 9-38

"Connect all of the arts through one intensity of mind." ⸻

The first note of a song, the actor's first appearance from behind the curtain; these are some of the most important moments in a *Noh* play; for they afford the greatest opportunity to lead the collective mind of the audience. If there is excess tension in the actor's body at the beginning, the stylized poses and singing of *Noh* become wooden and uninteresting. The only way to sustain interest, is to maintain the proper degree of intensity without tension.

Often the actor must maintain a pose for considerable periods of time, with only slow, measured changes in position. Though the actor's face and body may be largely concealed under a costume, he often holds a delicate paper fan, which vibrates visibly with any physical tremor or tension. Holding the fan with Ki, the actor can hold the tip perfectly calm, or use it as an expressive instrument (Figs. 9-39 and 40).

Zeami taught his students to connect all of the arts through one intensity of mind. That which connects the arts is the spirit, or Ki of the actor. This is what causes the actor to appear to be pulled in all directions, like a taut bow string. If this Ki is allowed to slacken, then the actor loses the audience, and suddenly looks very small or absurd. Though *Noh* appears otherworldy at first, a skilled actor can reveal in his performance, the depth and power of this world, and the essential unity of Man with the Universe.

Fig. 9-39

Fig. 9-40

Implications for Daily Life

In its command of space, value placed on stylized, as opposed to realistic expression, and the perspective it gives on Ki; the *Noh* drama has much to teach the West. *Noh* reveals the relativity and flexibility of time. It shows that faster is not necessarily better. Often the sensation of speed is created in a *Noh* performance, without the actors and muscians actually moving quickly at all. A Japanese proverb states that the beggar who hurries, receives but a meager portion at the end of the day. When we measure our lives strictly by the clock, we fail to recognize the importance of Ki. There are many resources in life, including time, money, information; but far more important than these is Ki, without which the others amount to nothing. If we can remain calm and unified in any situation, we will have ample energy to accomplish what we need to do, regardless of the time available. There is no need to hurry, if we are in control of ourselves.

Noh also shows us the importance of subtlety in communication. We can often express more by showing less. This does not mean that we must conceal that which is within us, but rather reveal it more effectively. When we express on the outside all that we feel on the inside, we look foolish. Speaking from a calm and unified posture, our words have more impact and dignity. Not needing to force our opinions on other people, we can afford to speak with restraint, and still be heard.

If we truly coordinate mind and body in daily life, then we become photogenic at any moment, whether or not we are aware of the camera. Learning to look dignified and strong in the unguarded moment is one of the aims of Ki training; but it is one that cannot be faked. We all reveal what we cannot conceal.

10. The Tea Ceremony

What is the Tea Ceremony?

In feudal Japan, rare tea bowls were highly prized among noblemen, who were willing to pay exorbitant prices to acquire them. In the sixteenth century lived a tea master, who by the age of fifty, had attained universal acclaim as one of the greatest masters of the art. His name was Sen-no-Rikyû. He was patronized by the most powerful feudal lord of Japan in his day, Toyotomi Hideyoshi; and accompanied him on military campaigns. Hideyoshi was a man who was enamored of displays of wealth and pomp. He used tea bowls and equipment fashioned of gold. Rikyû was a man at the other extreme; a man of quiet and refined taste. Rikyû was privy, no doubt, to many political secrets, because many such meetings were conducted under the guise of a Tea Ceremony. Most likely for political reasons, but apparently over a trivial disagreement, Hideyoshi ordered Rikyû to commit ritual suicide at the age of seventy, leaving behind him a tradition that still thrives today, with many followers around the world.

The tea ceremony is typically conducted in a small room, barely large enough to seat half-a-dozen people. While the etiquette has become formalized, and is quite complex, it was originally based on very simple principles. A highly refined sense of natural beauty is evident in everything from the manners of the guests, to the bowls and equipment used in preparing the tea. The tea itself is a rather thick, and slightly bitter liquid, prepared from young tea leaves, ground to a fine powder. It is served with traditional Japanese sweets, which are pleasing to the eye, and complement the bitterness of the tea.

In Japan today the majority of people who practice tea are women. Many of them study it as a sort of finishing school to polish etiquette before marriage. The Tea Ceremony has vastly limited itself in becoming so; as many men and women alike, have rejected it for its apparent fussiness and superficiality. But in feudal Japan, the Tea Ceremony was typically practiced by men only; and furthermore, by men of the warrior class, as a way of calming the mind before going into battle or making important decisions. There is much in Rikyû's approach that still suggests this original spiritual purpose, but it has been forgotten by many people who judge it as a mere pastime for the elite.

The tea ceremony is said to be difficult because of its many rules of etiquette, complex and difficult sequence of steps, which require both presence of mind and graceful movement. Yet anyone can learn these things with practice. What cannot necessarily be learned by practice, is the state of awakening or enlightenment, which the tea ceremony is supposed to be an expression of.

The dilemmas of tea are essentially the dilemmas of Zen. To live fully in the moment; to express the universe in a small quiet room; to fully open the mind in daily life; to live life with quiet strength.

How to Prepare Tea—The Short Ceremony

Before looking at how the Tea Ceremony develops and expresses Ki, it would be helpful to see what is actually done to prepare and serve tea. The sequence of the short version is explained here step by step. However, this is not intended to be a set of instructions on the method of preparing tea. Many important details are not highlighted here; and some things are very difficult to show in photographs.

First the tray, containing all of the necessary utensils, is set in front of the kettle and brazier (Fig. 10-1). The water disposal container is placed within easy reach by the left knee (Fig. 10-2). Then the napkin, which has been tucked in the sash of the *kimono* (着物), is taken and folded in the left hand (Fig. 10-3). Next, the napkin is used to wipe the surface of the tea caddy, which is then replaced, to the left of its original position (Fig. 10-4). The tea scoop is then cleaned in the same way, and set on the inside right edge of the tray (Fig. 10-5). Both the wooden tea scoop, and the lacquer caddy have already been cleaned before being brought in front of the guests. Using the napkin to wipe them clean before the guests, is a gesture with symbolic importance. It also helps to calm and focus the mind.

Next, the napkin is used to shut the lid of the kettle, which until now has been slightly ajar to let steam escape (Fig. 10-6). Great care must be taken to avoid being burned by the steam. Men are expected to perform this step without a napkin, with their bare fingers. Then the tea kettle is taken in the left hand, and hot water is poured into the tea bowl, to warm and clean it (Fig. 10-7). The tea whisk is taken and turned inside the hot water (Fig. 10-8). This not only cleans it, but seals its tiny pores, so that it will not be stained by the green tea later. Having replaced the tea whisk, the water in the tea bowl is then poured into the water disposal container at the left knee (Fig. 10-9).

The tea cloth, made of white linen or cotton, is then taken in the right hand (Fig. 10-10); opened out in one fold, and draped over the edge of the tea bowl (Fig. 10-11). The bowl is then rotated 3 1/2 times to wipe the edges. The inside of the bowl is then wiped four times with the moist cloth. The tea scoop is then taken in the right hand, and held above the right knee, while suggesting to the guests that they begin to partake of the Japanese tea cakes which have been set before them (Fig. 10-12).

The tea caddy is then taken in the left hand, and the lid removed with the right, while it still holds the tea scoop. The lid is placed on the edge of the tray, where the scoop was. The scoop is used to gather a generous amount of the finely powdered green tea, without spilling any prematurely, into the tea bowl (Fig. 10-13).

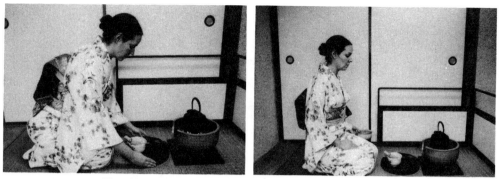

Fig. 10-1

Fig. 10-2

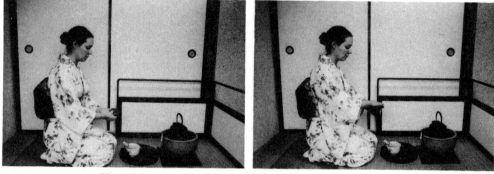

Fig. 10-3

Fig. 10-4

Fig. 10-5

Fig. 10-6

The tea is placed in the bowl, and any excess powder adhering to the scoop is gently knocked off. The lid is replaced on the caddy, which is then put back on the tray. The tea scoop is set where it had been, on the edge of the tray. The bottom of the bowl is filled with water, as before; in the formal thick tea ceremony, only enough for three or four sips, and the kettle and napkin are replaced in their original positions. The tea is then whisked by the forearm, until it makes a bright green frothy liquid (Fig. 10-14). The bowl of tea is then taken in the right hand, resting on the palm of the left (Fig. 10-15). The bowl is turned so that its appealing front faces the guests, and it is offered to the first guest (Fig. 10-16). At this point the guests give a salutation of respect, which is returned (Fig. 10-17).

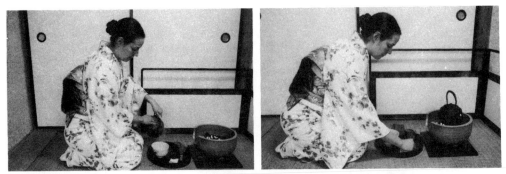

Fig. 10-7   Fig. 10-8

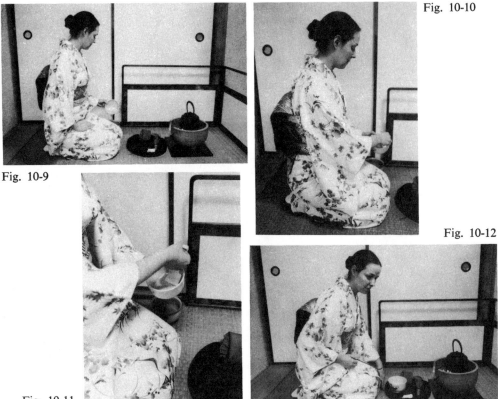

Fig. 10-10

Fig. 10-9

Fig. 10-12

Fig. 10-11

After the guest has consumed the tea and returned the bowl, the bowl is then replaced on the tray. The kettle is then taken as before, water poured into the bowl, the water disposed of, the bowl wiped clean, and the next guest served in turn. After the last guest has finished, the tea whisk is cleaned in the bowl (Fig. 10-18). Finally the tea cloth is placed in the bowl, and the tea whisk on top of it.

The napkin is once again unfolded (Fig. 10-19), and the tea scoop wiped clean of adhering tea powder (Fig. 10-20). The tea scoop is placed next to the whisk on the tea bowl (Fig. 10-21). The caddy is returned to its original central position in front of the bowl (Fig. 10-22). The adhering tea powder is gently brushed from the napkin into the water disposal container (Fig. 10-23). The lid of the tea kettle is once again set slightly ajar (Fig. 10-24). The napkin is folded for a final time,

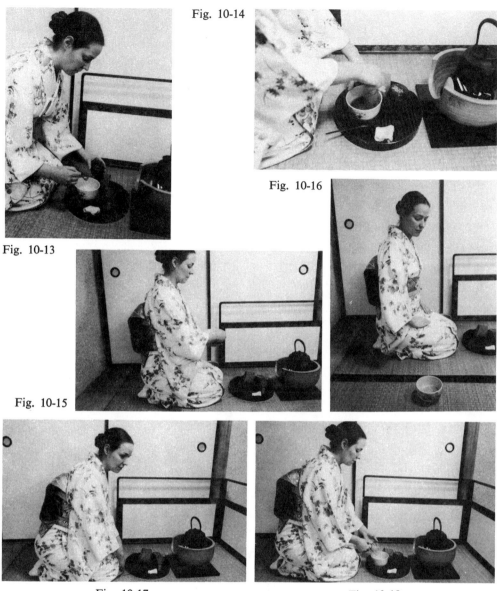

Fig. 10-14

Fig. 10-13

Fig. 10-16

Fig. 10-15

Fig. 10-17   Fig. 10-18

and tucked in the sash of the *kimono* (Fig. 10-25). The water disposal container is taken in the left hand (Fig. 10-26), and removed from the room. Then the host returns, removes the tray, and the ceremony concludes with a bow, and departure.

Though this concludes the ceremony, there is still much to be done in the preparation room. The cleaning equipment is often very valuable, and must be handled with great care. Even before the tea ceremony begins, until after it is completed, there must be no slackening in the Ki, or many technical aspects of the performance will suffer. All implements are placed within perfect reach, and the sequence is such that missing steps will tell. The biggest difference is evident in the taste and consistency of the tea itself. Careless or unskillful preparation may produce tea which is too lumpy, bitter, or too watery.

Fig. 10-19

Fig. 10-20

Fig. 10-21

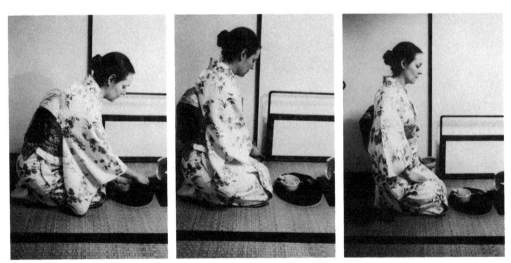

Fig. 10-22

Fig. 10-23

Fig. 10-26

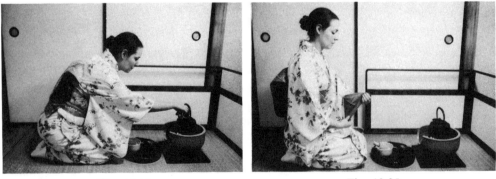

Fig. 10-24

Fig. 10-25

The Essential Teachings of Sen-no-Rikyû ————————————

Once one of Rikyû's disciples asked him what the most important things were to keep in mind at a tea gathering. Rikyû gave him seven simple principles, which seemed so obvious, that his student said that he already knew how to do those things. Rikyû claimed that if his student could host a tea ceremony without losing any of those principles, then Rikyû himself would become his student's disciple.

There are many things that we know or understand in theory, but cannot perform in practice. In other words, there are many things which we think we understand, but which have not penetrated deeply enough to become part of our subconscious mind, our second nature. Yet it is only in this realm that we can begin to coordinate mind and body. Rikyû's seven principles follow.

"Make the best possible bowl of tea." ————————————

When Ki is strong and the body relaxed, there is a quieting effect on the immediate environment. Calm and alert, the mind takes in and appreciates more. This is the real meaning of cultivating richness in simplicity, and the real purpose behind Tea Ceremony etiquette.

As convenient and necessary as they are, instant foods have robbed us of this sensibility. Most modern foods and drinks are manufactured on a scale which totally precludes the human touch. It does not necessarily disturb the mind to eat in this way; but unless we occasionally make time to take food and drink in the spirit of the Tea Ceremony, we are likely to forget how. For this, no complex etiquette or expensive equipment is required. Merely to eat and drink in a state of mind and body coordination is sufficient.

The handling of beautiful and valuable implements in the Tea Ceremony helps draw the mind to the fingertips. Tea bowls are made in many styles, and are selected for seasonal and aesthetic appropriateness (Fig. 10-27). The bowl is enjoyed for its shape, texture, and for the unique features endowed by its glaze. Some bowls are extraordinarily expensive; so much so, that etiquette calls for bowls to be held and appreciated near to the floor, in respect for their great value. The bright green

Fig. 10-27

frothy liquid swirling against a background of a lustrous black, rough-textured bowl, is a thing of great beauty.

The tea scoop is whittled from bamboo, which accounts for its jointed bend in the center. The whisk is also made of bamboo, with many fine, curved brush-like strips in the head (Fig. 10-28). The scoop contains no concave spoon-like portion, so care must be taken not to spill any of the fine powdered tea in the process of serving it. The fine brush tips of the whisk must be treated with care to avoid deforming their beautiful original shape. The tea in the bowl is shallow, only three or four sips. Yet care must be taken not to scrape the whisk along the bottom of the tea bowl. The whisk brushes the bowl with a feather touch, if at all. It is impossible to use either the tea scoop or whisk skillfully if there is any tension or distortion in the body.

The tea caddy itself is a work of art (Fig. 10-29). Like the tea bowls, they are made in a wide variety of shapes and designs. Some lacquered caddies are inlaid or sprinkled with gold. It is only used to contain tea during the ceremony. Usually the tea is stored in a tightly sealed container to preserve its freshness.

In the longer and more formal version of the Tea Ceremony, a long ladle is used to transfer water (Fig. 10-30). This too requires considerable skill to manipulate. The ladle must often be delicately balanced when it is set down, in one smooth motion, without stopping the arm or making any adjustments.

The best tea is made with human hands. When care is extended to all of the implements surrounding the preparation of tea, the taste of the tea naturally improves. But the greater responsibility of the tea host or hostess is to open the

Fig. 10-29

Fig. 10-28

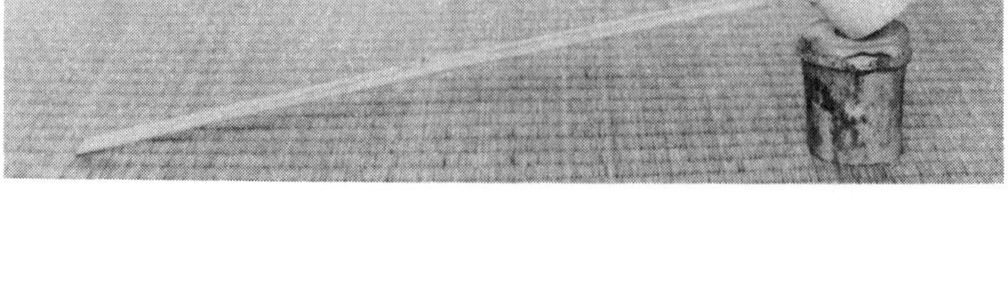

Fig. 10-30

minds of all present to the inherent beauty and grace of mind and body coordination.

"Arrange the charcoal so that it just boils the water, without wasting heat."

Rikyû himself was a master of detail. There is a story about his instructions to a carpenter, whom he was supervising in the building of a tea hut. A problem arose about where to put the nail for the hanging scroll in the recessed area, known as the *tokonoma* (床の間). Rikyû made him adjust the position so many times before driving the nail, that the carpenter grew impatient. Rikyû seemed impossible to satisfy; a fussy man with unreasonable standards. Just to test the master, the carpenter made a tiny mark on the wall, visible only to himself, and then pretended to drop the nail accidentally, losing the master's carefully selected place. Though Rikyû was sitting too far away to notice the tiny mark, he led him again in the same way to precisely the same spot on the wall.

This kind of precision and refined aesthetic sense is only possible for a person with a very calm and perceptive mind. The ideal of the Tea Ceremony is "flawless movement," or movement without any wasted effort. This goes down to the smallest detail, including the arrangement of the charcoal in the iron brazier. Yet this is not the cold efficiency of a mechanical process. The materials allow for tremendous variation. No two tea bowls, flower arrangements, or hanging scrolls are alike. Every new gathering of people, even of the same people, is totally unique.

Fig. 10-31

In a formal Tea Ceremony room, the brazier is set in a recessed portion of the floor. The placement of the scroll is a matter of fine aesthetic judgment, with an eye to asymmetrical balance (Fig. 10-31). Yet within this seemingly pristine setting, many things can go wrong. The process of preparing tea is a highly refined skill, and cannot be performed absent-mindedly. The proper amount of water must be added so that all of the tea will dissolve, and not leave small lumps of powder in the bowl. The tea napkin must be folded and unfolded with grace and control. A new guest may not know the proper way to sit, or may be restless about the proper etiquette. The host or hostess must be mindful of the needs and feelings of all of the guests, and perform a difficult series of delicate movements, all without losing composure. Because of the potential for variation and the unexpected, a student of tea must also be good at creative improvisation. The ability to skillfully manage the unexpected is one of the most highly prized qualities in a tea ceremony.

"Arrange the flowers as they are, to express their true nature."

There are several major schools of flower arranging, known as *ikebana* (生花). In their artifice, each of them stands apart from *chabana* (茶花), or tea flowers, in which a single flower is placed in such a way as to express the whole of nature through the part. Naturally the flowers are chosen in season, and express the atmosphere of nature month by month (Figs. 10-32, 33, and 34). Hideyoshi was so fond of artifice, that he greatly admired a small room literally filled to the brim with sprays of cherry blossoms. Simplicity is best, in all things, because it is free to express Ki, beyond form. Nature is dynamic and unquenchable, because it is constantly renewed by life's energy itself.

| Fig. 10-32   January | Fig. 10-33   April | Fig. 10-34   September |

Central to the aesthetic concepts of the Tea Ceremony is the expression of quiet strength. *Wabi* (侘) expresses the idea of austerity, or quiet taste. *Sabi* (寂) is similar, but suggests the elegance and refinement of something very simple, and very old. In their adjectival forms, as *sabishii*, and *wabishii*, both of these words have come to take on a rather negative nuance, meaning loneliness, or lack of resolve. In its negative meaning, these words describe the state of one who has lost the unity of mind and body. Their original meaning suggests just the opposite; one who truly feels the original unity of mind and body with the Universe cannot possibly be lonely or small minded.

Arranging the flowers as they are in the field means arranging them to express their essential unity with nature. As mere symbolism, this has little significance. Its real meaning is discovered in the experience of mind and body unity.

"In summer suggest coolness; in winter, warmth."

The first principle of tea ceremony aesthetics is balance. But this balance is peculiarly asymmetrical, always suggesting the dynamic interplay of opposites. All forms of Ki development express this balance of opposites: quiet strength. And this is often connected to the seasons. Bowls used in winter usually have a warm, self-contained quality, with nearly vertical walls (Fig. 10–35). By contrast, summer tea bowls have a wider, expanding lip, that suggests an open and cool feeling (Fig. 10-36). Japanese tea cakes are sweet, to balance the slightly bitter taste of the tea. They are served in very colorful arrangements, before the tea is taken. Here too, there is much variation, with attention given to monthly seasonal changes (Fig. 10–37).

Fig. 10-35   Fig. 10-36

October   August   November

Fig. 10-37

"Anticipate well, and be prepared."

Rikyû taught that the mind was first in everything. This could be expressed in many ways. He taught that one should always come early, and be ready. A person who is prepared can be ready to attend to the guests; can afford to be gracious.

There is a story of a Japanese frame maker's shop assistant, who was continually scolded by the shop owner for his forgetfulness. He never put tools back where they belonged. The things that he needed were never at hand. As a result, the shop was a mess, and he wasted much time and effort getting up and down out of his seat to look for tools. Gradually, over a two or three year period, he began to correct his sloppy habits, arranging things neatly on shelves, and gathering about him the necessary tools before beginning the day's work. The master of the shop was pleased, but puzzled about what had brought on this change in behavior. When he asked the shop assistant, he was told that the assistant had been studying the Tea Ceremony, and learned from it how to conduct his daily life and work.

The necessary implements are not only prepared before the Tea Ceremony, they are very much at hand (Fig. 10-38). Nothing gets in the way, and there is no need to get up or stretch to get something that is needed. It takes much practice to be able to sense just what the proper distance is, and in what sequence the most effortless and graceful movement occurs. Even in the preparation room, out of sight of the guests, everything is kept orderly and in place (Fig. 10-39).

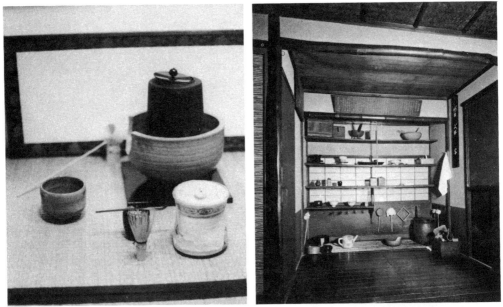

Fig. 10-38   Fig. 10-39

But merely keeping things orderly and at hand is of limited value without a corresponding state of mental readiness; an attentiveness that contains enough flexibility to respond well to the unexpected. Japanese do not wear shoes in the house. Shoes are neatly arranged in the waiting area next to the front door, facing outward so that they can easily be slipped on when departing. Careless people, with a rough and unrefined spirit, tend to cast off their shoes or slippers, leaving the waiting area in a disorderly state. Because the feet are the foundation of the body, care must be given to how the shoes are left. Otherwise it casts doubt on the character of the wearer.

"Bring an umbrella, even when the sky is clear." ─────────

Students of the Tea Ceremony are trained to move without wasted effort; giving attention to every movement of the hands and feet. Bringing an umbrella on a clear day is not to be understood as merely taking precautions, or being unwilling to take a chance. It refers more to a mental state which shows consideration for others; which is undisturbed by interruptions, because it is calm and ready.

At the end of the 17th century, a feudal lord from rural Japan was ordered to make his annual trip to the capital city of Edo. He insisted on being accompanied by his reluctant retainer, who was also a tea master. Though not a *samurai* by birth or training, the tea master was asked to dress as one, and carry a sword. While walking alone in the streets of Edo, he was accosted by a masterless *samurai*, who apparently recognized that the tea master had no military training, and hoped to easily rob him of some money by challenging him to a duel. The tea master apologized, saying that he was only dressed as a *samurai*, and was unprepared for a real fight. Renewed in his determination to rob the man of his money, the masterless *samurai* insisted on the duel.

On the pretext of wanting to get permission from his lord, he requested a short period of time, to prepare himself to die with dignity. He went to a sword master to be instructed in how to die without shame. The sword master asked him first to prepare tea. Thinking it his last time to perform the Tea Ceremony, he was able to bring to it his full self. The sword master's reaction was that there was no need for him to learn what he already knew. He instructed him to face the duel with the same frame of mind that he did in the Tea Ceremony, to hold his sword before him, and to strike his opponent at the same moment that he himself was struck. He predicted that it would end in death for both, and dignity for himself.

On the day of the duel, the tea master did as he was instructed, but the duel never took place; because the upstart *samurai* was unable to find an opening for his attack. He backed down in fear of what he saw in the tea master's figure.

Bringing an umbrella on a clear day is just this, a state of readiness and dignity, capable of showing the whole universe through a small part of it. It is reflected in our daily behavior. A person in this state of mind does not burst carelessly into a room without knocking. He or she takes measure of the atmosphere of the place, and of the depth of mind and body unity before entering a room. To do otherwise in a tea ceremony is not only rude, but may break something valuable, or interrupt something. But more important than the proper etiquette of opening the door, is that the person in a state of readiness calms the mind and extends Ki before entering a room or beginning a new task.

Although the Tea Ceremony appears to contain much delicacy and refinement, it also requires great internal strength. The tea bowl is held in the palm of the left hand, and supported by the right. It must be held with Ki, that is with the weight underside, the entire time; even while drinking. Though this Ki test should never be performed with a valuable tea bowl, your partner can test you by lifting up beneath your left hand (Fig. 10-40). If the mind and body are unified, then it will be very difficult for your partner to lift the bowl beyond where you want to hold it. The test can be sustained throughout the entire time that you drink, until you put the tea bowl back on the floor. As long as you maintain mind and body co-ordination, you should be easily able to drink and replace the bowl, and feel no sense of interference at all. You may be able to prevent the bowl from being lifted by resisting with strength; but the real test is in putting it back down. If there is any excess tension in your arms or upper body you will be unable to keep weight underside and put the bowl down where you choose. Or your body may fall over backwards as you drink from the cup. For this reason it is best to practice with a durable and inexpensive ceramic piece.

Fig. 10-41

Fig. 10-40

Fig. 10-42

All implements in the tea ceremony must be handled in a similar way, although it is inappropriate to test someone during a Tea Ceremony. The same principle applies as well to any cup that we drink from; even if it is made from plastic and held in one hand. If we hold a cup casually, without keeping our mind on what we are doing, then it can easily be knocked out of our hand, and spilled in our lap, when the hand is hit from below (Fig. 10-41). However even when the strike is un-expected, if the weight is underside, the cup will naturally fly away from you, in the direction of the person who tried to make you spill it (Fig. 10-42). All of this occurs without any conscious effort or aiming on your part. It works just as well with the eyes closed.

One purpose of the Tea Ceremony is to purify and refresh the mind. The reason that the mind becomes cluttered and polluted with the concerns of daily life, is that our Ki extension is not strong enough to wash them away. When we try to hold Ki back inside ourselves, we lose the power to resist all sorts of minor shocks and influences. Small things irritate us and get under our skin. But if Ki extension is strong, it will naturally repel negative influences; improving our resistance to disease, accidents, and negative attitudes. When performed with mind and body unity, the tea ceremony is all that its early masters claimed it could be.

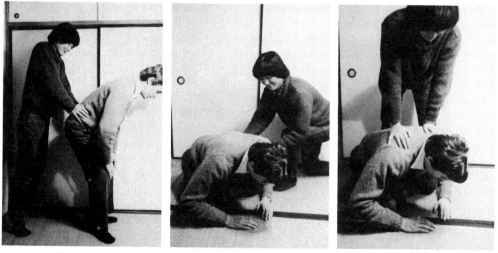

| Fig. 10-43 | Fig. 10-44 | Fig. 10-45 |

Tea Ceremony etiquette is often misunderstood, even by those who practice it. Merely bowing as a gesture of social etiquette is a hollow ritual. A true bow is large and strong, but silent. It is performed with a single, graceful stroke. Stand in a natural posture with mind and body unified, feet slightly apart. The standing bow is performed in one simple stroke, bending the knees and lowering the One Point, until the palms rest gently on the knees. There is no need to change the position of the head, neck, or eyes. The bowing pose is held for a moment or two, and then you simply return to the original standing position. Assume the standing bowing position, and ask your partner to push with both hands on your hips, on a 45-degree angle, in an attempt to make you lose your balance. If done correctly, this posture is very stable (Fig. 10-43). If you bow with the knees stiff and the chin jutted forward, looking ahead at the person to whom you are bowing, the posture is not only very rude, but very unstable.

The seated bow is also performed in a single beautiful stroke. Sit in the *seiza* position, with hands completely relaxed, resting on the thighs, each facing in at about 45 degrees. In bowing forward, the hands simply slide down the thighs, until the forefingers and thumbs make a triangle on the ground in front of the knees. At the same time, the upper body bends forward as a unit, as in the standing position, so that the forehead is above the triangle, at a height of about two widths of the fist. The return to the seated, *seiza* position is made in the same way, in the reverse direction. Hold the bowing position long enough to allow your partner to try to push you over, by placing both hands against your rib cage, and pushing at right angles (Fig. 10-44). When done correctly, this position is surprisingly strong, immovable as a rock. Before returning to the seated position, ask your partner to try to keep you down by pushing down from above on both of your shoulders (Fig. 10-45). Without any sense of effort, you should be able to return to the *seiza* position, because all of your partner's Ki is absorbed at your One Point.

The same tests can be applied to the bowing posture done incorrectly, that is with tension in the shoulders. When tested from the side, you are likely to fall over. When tested with full body weight from above, pushed on your shoulders, you will be unable to rise, even though you push off of the ground with your hands. However if you bow from the One Point, and simply return on the same arc, you will not even feel the weight of a heavy person. The Japanese character for the word, "etiquette," suggests showing respect to the spirit of something. Bowing with mind and body unified is more than a social gesture, and more than a gesture of humility. It shows respect for the other, while developing strong Ki within the self.

"Direct your full attention to your guests." ————

It is proverbial in Japan that there is room for respect, even among close friends. The word for human being is *ningen* (人間), written with the characters for person, and interval or space. A tea gathering is a chance to reaffirm this space and respect between all people, and all things of value, without which their identity would be lost and unappreciated. At the same time, it is an opportunity to open the mind, and meet close friends heart to heart. Students of the Tea Ceremony are encouraged to enlarge their circle of tea friends for this reason. Of course the Tea Ceremony can easily be performed without this spirit, as a way of trying to impress, or as a mere display of archaic formal etiquette. This is the Tea Ceremony which most foreigners encounter when they visit Japan as tourists. Many young Japanese women in the 20th century have studied Tea Ceremony merely to add another credential to their marriage eligibility portfolio, or so that they may entertain their husband's business guests. This kind of Tea Ceremony is a pale imitation of what Rikyû conceived of and practiced in the 16th century.

The expression made famous by the tea ceremony, *Ichigo* (一期), *ichie* (一会), meaning "One time, One meeting," was popularized by the *samurai* who practiced Tea Ceremony in medieval Japan. As the outcome of the next fight was always unsure, it became their practice to act as if each tea meeting may be their last. Alongside this developed the preference for non-verbal, yet very direct communication; an ability which is still respected in Japan today. Etiquette was highly formalized, so it left plenty of room for trying to intuit how the other person felt, or

Fig. 10-46

what they meant, judging only from slight variations in posture or tone of voice. In this way, practitioners of the Tea Ceremony became excellent judges of sincerity and intent.

Rikyû summarized the spirit of a tea gathering in four words, written here by the contemporary headmaster of the Rikyû's school of Tea, Sen-no-Soshitsu: *wa kei sei jaku* (和敬静寂) (Fig. 10-46). *Wa* means peace, unity, or harmony. It can also mean to soften, or calm down. *Kei* suggests respect, honor, and veneration. It also conveys a sense of distance. *Sei* means to purify, or cleanse. That which leaves no trace of itself is pure. *Jaku* means quiet; mellow, solitary, and still. It is bringing these concepts to life through one's body and movements, in the process of preparing and serving tea, that makes the Tea Ceremony a highly developed form of Ki training.

Implications for Daily Life

The Tea Ceremony teaches us to live fully in the present. It shows us how to take food and drink in the spirit of appreciation and humility, without losing dignity. It was at one time considered very rude in Japan to eat or drink while walking. Doing many things at once; hurrying without taking care; overeating or eating while upset; these things disturb the mind and injure the health. Nervous habits, like chewing gum, or mindlessly eating while watching television do us harm; because they gradually rob us of the ability to focus and clarify our mind when it counts.

PART III

Thriving
in the World
of Change

11. Presence of Mind

The Importance of Having a Purpose

The word "crisis" is derived from a Greek term, meaning decisiveness, or point of decision. A crisis is a situation that literally demands presence of mind. A person who responds to a crisis reflexively, in fight or flight, is considered an animal; guided by instincts alone. The least intelligent response is paralysis. All living things respond more or less to the environment in which they live. Whether large or small, a crisis is a dividing point; a test of response. The greater the presence of mind, the more successful the response.

A decision is actually a goal; a mental picture of the desired result. Without clear goals, we have no means of interpreting the feedback which we get from our environment. The noise of the world is so great, that it tends to upset and scatter the mind. When the mind is calm and clear, Ki naturally becames very strong. Like the morning sun, it dispels the darkness and mist which obscures our path.

Whether riding a bicycle, threading a needle, or solving a problem, even our performance in very small things depends on having a clear picture of the desired result, and appropriate feedback on how we are doing. Most of the tasks of daily life involve well established routines, and activities which we can perform semi-automatically. Things which we do well, we take for granted. But when the pressure is great, or the risks high, then most people lose their presence of mind. Anyone can walk a straight line on the ground; not many people can walk on a steel girder in a high rise building under construction. Anyone can talk comfortably to a friend, but few can speak before a large audience.

The pressure and sense of risk which inhibits our ability to learn and perform is highly subjective. Fear and self-consciousness often inhibits people from performing what to another would be a perfectly normal task. The ability to speak is something often taken for granted, yet speaking before others strikes enough fear in some people to make them stutter uncontrollably. Stuttering comes from forcing the mouth to move without a clear mental image of what one wants to say. When the mind is preoccupied with fear of losing control, that itself becomes an inadvertent goal, leading the body to produce the result visualized so fearfully in the mind. Even a normal speaker can be made to stutter if he is forced to listen to his own voice with a moment's delayed feedback. And stutterers will tend to speak normally if they are forced to listen to a loud tone that drowns out their own voice. People born deaf rarely speak well, because they receive no aural feedback on their own speech, and they have no clear mental image of what speech sounds like. We are all better speakers when we feel strongly about a topic. Presence of mind reduces the sense of fear which otherwise inhibits our ability and enjoyment of whatever we do.

Goals are mental pictures; imaginary experiences of an idealized result. The actual result is always only an approximation of the ideal. But the clearer the goal, the closer the approximation. Because the goal is inevitably somewhat vague at first, we rarely achieve our goals the first time we try. It is essential to have at all times a written statement of what you want in life. But writing it on paper is not carving it in stone. Your goals naturally change over time. This statement, or list of goals must be reviewed and refined on a daily basis. No matter how major the task or distant the goal, it can always be broken down into smaller intermediate steps. Merely thinking about it is not enough. Goals are usually vague in thought. Only by writing them down, reviewing and rewriting them, can we bring them into focus. It takes time, trial and error, and practice to refine and sharpen the mental images of what we want to be and do. The mind-set taken at the beginning of any task is very important. We should set our sights beyond what we think we can accomplish as individuals. Ki itself is not limited, and it is this Ki which leads our body into action. If we extend strong Ki, we will be able to think and aspire beyond the limitations which restrict us now. Then, even if we only accomplish half as much as we aim for, it will still be beyond what we once thought possible.

Meanwhile we are bombarded by feedback from the people and things around us. How we interpret and use this feedback depends on how clear and calm the mind is.

Presence of mind is self-awareness: a unified mind and body with a clear sense of purpose. Feedback on performance is necessary and unavoidable. But it is no substitute for a clear goal. Excessive carefulness and self-criticism merely inhibits Ki. Negative feedback tells us that we are off-course. It tells us to modify our direction, not to stop altogether. A bicycle can only remain upright as long as it is in motion. Yet it is always in the process of losing and regaining balance. When first learning to ride, a child has no clear image of how or what to do. If the child is motivated to learn, then trial and error will gradually produce more subtle responses to the sensation of losing balance, and the fear of falling will drop away.

Ki tests are designed to provide biofeedback on the goal of mind and body unification. There is no machine which can directly measure Ki. Nor is one needed, because the body is the visible portion of the mind. Ki tests and exercises are a valuable means of training the subconscious mind and developing strong Ki. However it is not always convenient or possible to perform them in the midst of our daily affairs. Regular practice under a qualified instructor will help you to internalize the feedback that the tests provide. It is also necessary to find ways to check yourself throughout the day. But as important as these self-checks are, they are ultimately no more than a supplement to Ki training. Without a clear idea of what Ki is, it is impossible to learn to discriminate the real thing from an imitation. Sugar and salt look alike. But when you actually taste them, you can easily tell them apart. Words are even more deceptive. Some people with no Ki training whatsoever, use the word Ki quite freely. Some of the things that they teach and say are not consistent with the ideas in this book. The most reliable way to learn Ki is to take nothing for granted. Refine and develop your own understanding of Ki, testing your insights as you go, by trial and error. Determine to find the real thing for yourself, and others will recognize the genuine article in you.

Posture and Body Language

One way to check mind and body coordination without testing it, is to observe posture and body language. Your sensitivity will improve with Ki development. This sense stays with you. Mirrors and photographs can help us to see ourselves as others do. But don't just stop at physical appearances. Develop an eye to see the part that is not visible: the Ki. Mirrors allow us to make adjustments, which is why vain people enjoy them. Photographs catch us as we were at a particular moment. Casual photographs are particularly revealing. Develop strong Ki in daily life; and learn to become photogenic from the point of view of mind and body coordination.

It is not necessary to be aloof or elitist about mind and body coordination. A unified posture is not a pose. It is the most natural and the strongest posture. There is no standard posture to which all should conform. However, it is very difficult to maintain mind and body unification in a casual posture, if you have not first mastered it in a more formal, fundamental posture. People should not be judged according to their level of mind and body unity if they are ignorant about it. Quick learners will eagerly absorb what you have to show them. But even if the topic never comes up, people will notice and respond differently to you when your posture is unified. There are plenty of people who want to learn. Don't waste your time trying to teach it to those that don't.

The unified posture and way of moving is covered in detail in Part I. Previous chapters contain plenty of material to help you refine and sharpen your mental image of mind and body unity. It is also helpful to know how to recognize common examples of the lack of mind and body unity. When you find them in yourself, you can adjust accordingly. When you find it in others, you have to use judgment about how and whether to respond. This requires sensitivity, because most people are not interested in changing themselves. Others react negatively to new things which they don't understand. The most effective way to help others is to be a good example yourself. Then its value will become apparent to others, and they will ask you for help.

Watch people when they stand. When the mind is restless, the feet are rarely still. Shifting nervously back and forth, the weight rarely settles on the balls of the feet. This is one reason why public speakers stand behind a podium: to conceal nervous foot movements which can be seen by the whole audience. Lack of mind and body coordination creates anxiety; a subconscious feeling that one is falling apart. People respond to this in different ways. Some try to hold themselves together by keeping their hands in their pockets; or by crossing and folding their arms. This can be done without losing One Point, but is usually a result of loss of the unified posture.

The lack of mind and body coordination becomes even more pronounced in movement. Walking reveals this very clearly, with endless variations. The rhythm and weight of the footsteps tells a lot. People who lack purpose often walk glancing back frequently over their shoulders. Or they sway from side to side as they walk, rather than striding along upright. Tension in the shoulders greatly reduces the mobility of the arms; so much so that a person may not even be aware that one, or even both arms don't swing freely. The arm may hang limply at the side, even while walking. Such people often cut a sad figure when viewed from behind. Excess tension is also visible in the way people carry things. This is one reason why eating while walking is considered bad manners: it is almost impossible to do both things gracefully at the same time. Carrying a package or briefcase close to the body, or tucked up under the upper arm is very tiring and inefficient. It is an indication that the weight is upperside.

Standing and walking require at least some energy; but anyone can collapse into a comfortable chair without having mind and body unified. Many chairs are so poorly designed that they make it nearly impossible to sit correctly. Even though the chair feels quite comfortable, the weight is probably back too far. This causes the arms to strain forward in the shoulder joint, creating fatigue: hence the arm rest.

Other signs of fatigue include sitting or chewing with the chin jutting forward; particularly if the mouth is open. It is almost impossible to keep One Point in this posture. People who habitually sit like this cannot be relied on in a crisis, because they surprise easily and cannot move quickly. They take too long to pull themselves together. Though they rest frequently, it rarely refreshes them.

Frequent blinking is also a sign of weak Ki. Oversensitivity to sunlight means that the eyes are slow to adapt to light variations. A person with strong Ki can look briefly at the sun without blinking. However, this should not be done carelessly, as forcing the eyes to stare at the sun has been known to cause blindness.

Even in sleep, posture and body language can reveal lack of mind and body unity. In sleep the subconscious mind expresses itself freely, without self-conscious interference. Sleeping with the mouth open is a sign of mind and body disunity, as in waking. Tension expresses itself in restless body movements. Neurotic people tend to sleep with their arms folded and ankles crossed. Total relaxation in sleep is essential for restoring Ki. Regardless of the number of hours of sleep one gets, restless sleep is a sign of insufficient Ki. For such people, thirty minutes of Ki breathing or meditation just before going to bed is easily worth an extra hour or two of sleep.

When poor habits of posture and movement go uncorrected for a period of time, they leave traces of distortion in the body. The longer they go uncorrected, the more difficult they are to correct. If nothing is done, these habits ultimately result in physical deformities and diseases that are normally associated with old age. Chronological age plays a far less important role in this than lack of mind and body coordination in daily life. You can be young at sixty or old at thirty.

Lack of mind and body unification creates anxiety. In extreme cases, nervous tension heightens into fear. Though fear is usually associated with some external condition; heights, injury, criticism; it is essentially an unpreparedness for stress. Without a calm mind and strong Ki, we feel we have no control over events. Even the mere possibility of something going wrong can paralyze a person who is dominated by anxiety. Fear creates a desire for self-protection; usually in the form of a fight or flight reaction. Neither, are very effective in a crisis. The mind in conflict cannot free itself, without first putting an end to the storm within.

Fear Attracts Danger

Despite the fears people have of random street crime, most violent crimes are perpetrated by people who know, or are related to each other. Contacts with these people afford the greatest opportunities for friction; and social restraints can cause feelings to become dangerously repressed, until they explode in a violent act. The majority of people have enough self-control to avoid this. The crime that is most feared is that of random street violence; particularly as it seems to occur more and more often in places where it is least expected. The question to ask, is whether or not this violence is random.

In the late 1970s, a study was done on the non-verbal signals of vulnerability that pedestrians unwittingly convey to potential muggers. Sixty, short video-taped segments were taken of people walking in a dangerous section of New York City's garment district, using a hidden camera. An equal number of men and women of various ages were selected at random. None of them knew that they were being filmed during the six or seven seconds that it took them to pass the camera.

The tapes were taken to Rahway Prison in New Jersey, and shown to inmates convicted of violent crimes, including murder. The inmates rated each of the people on the tapes, as to the amount of resistance that they would expect to get from that person if they attempted an assault. The ratings were made on a scale which was developed in their own street language, by some of the inmates themselves. The main difference between those selected as victim or non-victim types, was not in age, body size, or sex; it was in their way of moving and walking.

The victim types tended to lift their feet when walking; whereas the non-victim types would swing their feet as they walked. Careful studies of the tapes by dance movement analysis also revealed that the victims were more likely to move in a disjointed or uncoordinated manner; the parts seeming to move separately from the whole. The non-victim types moved in a more fluid, coordinated fashion; as if moving from the center of the body. Further movement studies showed that certain styles of high-heeled shoes actually produce the very style of walking which the inmates would have selected as belonging to an easy victim.

The point is clear. Without any self-defense training at all, walking with mind and body coordinated is itself a powerful form of self-defense. As none of the pedestrians knew that they were being filmed, this was a realistic simulation of what happens when a street punk sizes up a potential victim.

The situation may change when the person knows that he or she is being watched or followed. A kid on the street who is contemplating violence, is likely to look for an easy victim, or a challenge. Sheep are easy victims; they can be taken without a struggle. Tigers may fight back, but a young gang can win points for taking out a tiger; and a direct challenge becomes a matter of saving face. Goat types are ambiguous. They don't look particularly strong or weak. If they fight back, and you lose, it looks very bad. Still, they don't look like they would give up easily. So goats survive on the street.

The Danger of Self-Defense

Self-defense is a double-edged sword, capable of cutting both the attacker and the victim. The problem with handguns, chemical sprays, and any other weapon that a person might carry for self-protection, is that so many things can go wrong. A gun can be taken away and used against you. A spray chemical directed at an attacker's face can blow back into your own face if the wind is against you. There is rarely time to consider these possibilities in a crisis. And the very display of a weapon on your part can so infuriate an attacker, that you may wind up far worse off than if you had remained calm. Furthermore, small children occasionally get hold of household guns, and accidentally use them on siblings in play.

Lessons in self-defense may seem to be a practical and safe alternative. However, it is impossible to really simulate a serious threat on the street, when practicing with friends and fellow students whom you must be careful to avoid injuring. The law is likely to favor the other side if you strike first, even in self-defense. Martial arts training can make a person aware of subtle non-verbal signals that precede an attack; but if the student's mind is not calm, he is likely to misinterpret any sign of tension as an imminent attack. Striking the other before he may, or may not strike you, is not only poor martial arts practice; it is against the law. As the apparent aggressor, you may easily go to jail for something that you did not start.

A good martial artist does not fight on the street; not because he is unable, but because his presence of mind never invites or arouses an attack.

Alternatives to Fighting

One may choose to fight, or not. One may win or lose. Of these, the worst indignity is to lose without fighting. The way most in accord with Ki principles is to win without fighting.

There are many ways to do this, if one remains calm enough to recognize all of the options. We often invite or provoke an attack, from our way of moving or responding to a threat. If you are accosted on the street, you can be fairly sure that you were carefully watched before being approached. What you cannot be sure of, is whether or not there are hidden friends of the attacker nearby to assist or stand guard.

Carrying a weapon, studying techniques of self-defense, or even thinking about what you would do in a hypothetical situation may all provide a sense of security; but it is a false one. There are no rules, and there are no precedents. Literally, anything can happen. This is a terrifying prospect to a person whose mind is gripped with tension, because he or she feels powerless to do anything about it.

However the inherent ambiguity of the situation is actually one's greatest resource. The criminal is not likely to be a paid assassin, whose job it is to kill you without warning. Anyone who is committing a crime has a certain amount of anxiety over getting caught. And chances are good that the attacker has a limited or unclear objective, far short of what he may be forced or scared into doing by your panicked response. The Japanese word for crisis suggests both danger and opportunity. How the situation turns out depends on how well you maintain your presence of mind, or Ki.

As long as you are not hypnotized by the attacker's threat or weapon, then your eyes will remain open to whatever options may present themselves. As every situation is unique, it is not particularly useful to try to memorize strategies for dealing with a particular situation. It may be appropriate to fight, or to flee with all of your might. The other person may be taken off-guard by your attempt to negotiate or reason with him. Humor or surprise may defuse the tension; psychologically disarm the aggressor. Or it may be appropriate to do nothing at all, as time may be on your side.

I know people who have escaped unharmed from potentially dangerous situations by simply remaining relaxed and being themselves. Others have managed to walk away unchallenged, by acting like they are mentally retarded. Rapes have been avoided by women claiming to have venereal disease, as there is no way for a rapist to be sure. However, an obvious bluff or transparent trick is not likely to work. Nothing is more ineffective in such a situation than failed or rehearsed surprise.

People are capable of doing things well beyond their ordinary limitations when they act with mind and body unified. A man or woman of very ordinary strength may be able to lift a 1,000 pound telephone pole, or the corner of an automobile which is pinning a person beneath. Or a person may accidentally walk out of a store, forgetting to pay for a small item, unnoticed by the store security people. If such a person had tried to shoplift, he would have been caught in a minute. It is when we think we know our strength that we begin to have problems.

At the same time, there is no need to deliberately flirt with danger. Walking alone at night in a dangerous neighborhood, or hitchhiking on a dark country highway are only asking for trouble, if such places can be avoided. Still, if you unavoidably find yourself in such a situation, the most effective thing you can do to ensure your own safety is to coordinate mind and body, and trust the Universe to give you no situation that you cannot deal with.

A successful burglar in 12th century China was asked by his son, the secret of his trade. The father told the son that it was time that he learned the art, and promised to show him the secret. The son accompanied his father as they broke into the house of a wealthy merchant, late at night. Without waking anyone up, the father managed to pick the lock on the treasure house door. Once his son was inside the room with all of the treasures, his father slammed the door on him, locked him inside, and then quickly slipped away before the household could catch him.

Meanwhile the son was locked inside the treasure room; the first place that the merchant and his servants came to check. Holding a candle-burning lantern in one hand, the merchant unlocked the door to the room and flung it open. The burglar's son blew out the candle and dashed out into the darkness, closely followed by the merchant and his men, who sounded the alarm for help to apprehend and kill the thief.

As the burglar's son ran by a well on the grounds, he tried to create a diversion by throwing down it a large stone; and then ran off in the darkness. His pursuers naturally heard the splash, and assumed that the thief had fallen in. As they gathered around the well congratulating themselves, the burglar's son made off into the night. When he returned home, he demanded to know the meaning of his father's action. The father agreed to explain it, after hearing in detail how his son managed to escape. As he told his story, he began to realize the valuable lesson that his father had taught him. In the face of a crisis, presence of mind is the best teacher.

Fear is Lack of Presence of Mind

Self-defense is always a very limited prospect. Survival entails a whole commitment of body and mind. But self-defense is an illusion entertained by the mind, to ease its anxiety over its lack of unity with the Universe. A frightened person, locked within his home, and armed in the event of encountering an intruder, is not alive; he is already half-dead. A suit of armor does provide a limited form of protection. But it also invites attack; and there is no defense yet invented that can not be penetrated.

The truth of the matter is, that no mortal can defend himself against everything forever. We can contribute to, or accelerate our own demise, but we cannot postpone it indefinitely. This realization only causes despair in the person who has lost trust in the original unity of mind and body. Strong Ki has strong survival value, because Ki is the life force itself. Extend Ki well, maintain good presence of mind, and the Universe will protect you. As long as we live, we should fill our lives with life, rather than fret and worry over death and injury.

Fear of all the things that could go wrong disturbs the mind, and cuts off the supply of fresh Ki from the Universe. Training in survival and problem solving, ensures that we won't take a naive or foolish approach to the matter of our own safety. It can also show us the simple fact that fear is counter-productive. Fear is lack of presence of mind. Like prayer in reverse; fear tends to attract the very thing that it would avoid. This is particularly true when it comes to the matter of defending one's body against criminal attack and abuse. Fear shrinks the mind and body; drains it of life. It acts like the taste of blood to the shark. The safest attitude is one which is firmly grounded in mind and body unity; and can therefore trust the Universe to protect it.

You Have Nothing to Lose—Until You Give Up

The world is full of people who complain of their lot, but do nothing to improve it. Idle complaining is a form of resignation from life. The more you indulge in it, the weaker you become. Yet many people genuinely feel powerless in the face of their bosses, families, or governments. Only occasionally does one meet a person who seems to defy all of the odds, and manage to pull through. I met such a person recently in Japan.

He was a professional Karate instructor, who had barely one year before, begun training in Aikidô and Ki, including Ki breathing. Just five months before I met him, he had been in a nearly fatal automobile accident, which no one should have been able to survive. He was thrown from his motorcycle at a high speed, when it was crushed between the car that had suddenly stopped in front of him, and the truck which was unable to stop behind him. He was thrown about ten meters, over the top of the car in front of him; which ran over him as it skidded to a stop. Another car swerved and ran over him a second time. When the ambulance picked him up, his skull was fractured like a jigsaw puzzle; his face was swollen and marred beyond recognition; his left arm had been severed; and he had suffered rib and leg fractures.

Neither the police, the ambulance crew, nor the doctors, gave him any serious prospect of survival. At best, he would live for a year or so, as a human vegetable in a wheel chair. The family had been gathered, and arrangements for the funeral were already underway. A day later he regained consciousness, although he was unable to do anything but stare at the hospital ceiling. His relative's children were terrified at the mere sight of his swollen and disfigured face.

His left arm had been reattached by a metal pin; though he was hardly aware of the total extent of his devastation. He felt somehow that he had been spared for a reason, or that he had something that he yet needed to accomplish in his life. He was unable to move a finger, but managed to breathe more or less regularly; so he decided to practice Ki breathing as much as he could, several hours per day.

To the doctor's amazement, he was able to sit up in bed within a month; and soon the scabs fell from his face and the swelling subsided, without leaving any scars. Only four months after the accident, he walked out of the hospital unassisted.

Five months after the accident, I met him at an Aikidô training camp in the

Fall of 1985. He participated in nearly every part of the camp; avoiding falls however, on his left side. I worked with him as a partner, before I knew anything of his story, and never suspected a word of it. I knew that he had only done Aikidô for a few months; and felt that his Ki was remarkably strong for a beginner.

The person who can truly come to terms with the fear of bodily harm or criminal molestation, is freed of a terrible burden. Even when there is no threat of personal danger, a person who projects the confidence born of mind and body unity, will make a strong impression on others. Likewise, the person who lives under the shadow of fear of physical injury, lives like a sacred dog; broadcasting to all concerned, that this is a person who doesn't complain when stepped on. The consequences of this attitude are far reaching. Your body language can open or close your options. It colors the tone of all human relationships. But this does not mean that we should swagger, or act boastfully. Though this may intimidate some, it is no more than the posturing of a weak person. Having a clear sense of purpose; keeping your mind on what you are doing; coordinating mind and body in your daily life will provide the right balance of strength and relaxation, and will help you shed your fear, and regain presence of mind.

12. Expanding Your Mental Horizons

Help Comes to Those who Help Themselves

The essence of the victim mentality is the belief that things are basically beyond your control. The anxiety that this produces may express itself in terms of a specific fear, such as fear of being attacked on the street, or losing one's job. There are so many things on which to place the blame: one's background or education; parents, teachers; the boss, the economy, the government. It is easier to believe that the mess you are in is not of your own making. People who are confused and disoriented usually look around for an enemy to blame, whether it is an individual, an institution, or the Devil himself.

Believing that they are powerless to solve their own problems, they accept things as they are, without trying to change or improve them. And there are usually plenty of other weak people who will accept and support them in their beliefs.

It requires a certain independence to shed this weak mentality, and to outgrow the state of extreme dependence. The essence of Ki development is growth. Ki itself cannot be contained; in fact it grows stronger when it meets resistance. This is the reason for Ki tests, and the rationale behind all of the problems and dilemmas posed to the student of the traditional arts of Japan. By contrast, the victim mentality finds it easy to accept and identify with the status quo. People who don't accept the status quo are sure to meet resistance from it. This very resistance requires you to expand your capacity to deal with it.

Ki principles teach that we have no enemy, because we are one with the Universe. This means that what we really have to overcome is not something external, but something inside ourselves. Once we stop fighting with ourselves, then we can learn to stop fighting with each other, and begin to solve the problems of the world. If we truly are one with the Universe, then its entire resources are at our disposal. Whether or not we accept this concept intellectually, each person will test and prove it in experience.

The dilemma is, that if we are one with the Universe, and if we do have its resources at our disposal; then why don't things appear that way? Why don't things go as well as they should?

The answer is that God, or the Universe, helps those who help themselves. All we need is initiative. The material resources of the world are dwindling. The only vastly underdeveloped resource remaining in the world, is the human mind. Even a genius is said to use no more than a small fraction of the brain's inherent potential. Activity and problem solving create opportunities for growth. But without initiative, there is no activity and no development.

What Limits Human Potential?

There are three factors which determine the limits of human potential. The first factor is knowledge or information. The second is experience; what we have learned, and the perspective that it gives us on our life. The third factor is Ki; the life force within us that gives us initiative to grow and solve problems.

Everyone has some degree of knowledge and experience. Both accumulate naturally with age. Though one person may make efforts to gain more than another, both information and learning are finite; there are limits on how much anyone can absorb. Only the third factor, Ki or initiative, is unlimited and freely available to anyone. Like factors in an equation, these three are multiplied together to produce a result. Knowledge and experience help, as do other finite resources, like money or time. But the one that can really make a significant difference is Ki. If Ki is weak, the end result will be insignificant. If Ki is absent, the other resources will amount to nothing.

We are born into a set of circumstances. Some people are better off than others. But sometimes it makes little difference in the end, whether or not you start out with wealth and power in the beginning. Success can be defined in many ways. No single way is right for all people. Success in anything requires some knowledge, some experience, and a tremendous amount of initiative. Without strong Ki, it is impossible to overcome the inertia of people and circumstances which would rather not see you succeed. If you succeed in overcoming your own self-imposed limitations, then you no longer have an excuse to lay the blame elsewhere.

The person who succeeds in surpassing himself, automatically puts pressure on others around him. Without this pressure, without examples of excellence in our lives, we would fade away in mediocrity. The function of a teacher of Ki development is to strive to use this pressure in a positive way, to inspire others to expand their capabilities and realize their potential. The great failure of modern education is that it fills people with information and learning, but stifles initiative. The measure of a teacher, manager, or any mentor, is the degree to which he or she shows others how they can surpass themselves.

Overcoming Inertia

Inertia is the tendency for an object at rest to stay at rest; or if moving in a certain direction, to continue in that direction. Life itself is in a constant state of change. To survive and grow in an environment of change, we must learn to overcome our inertia, and adapt to the demands of growth. The victim mentality is a kind of spiritual inertia; a refusal to accept and participate in life.

As soon as we stop extending strong Ki, things begin to go badly. If we cut our Ki long enough, we feel lost, out of place. Our judgment becomes poor and we lose our sense of timing. One can easily feel the tension in a group or organization where this has happened. It lacks a sense of coordinated purpose, and the chemistry between people is somehow wrong. Sometimes all the group needs is a leader with strong Ki, one who can inspire and motivate the others to overcome their inertia. A really sick person or organization will actively work to stifle initiative, in an effort to maintain the status quo.

Many problems are inherently ambiguous. They don't come with a set of ready-made instructions on how to solve the problem. People who lack initiative find this ambiguity intolerable. Still, anxiety doesn't make the problem go away. We experience this ambiguity as a problem that we are powerless to solve, because we stop questioning it. Parents, teachers, or managers may try to fix the situation by using force, or giving orders. This only works on people who want to be told what to do. Even while they complain, they cooperate willingly. In maintaining the status quo, they preserve their spiritual inertia. There are three kinds of people in the world: those who make things happen; those who watch things happen; and those who wonder what happened.

Using Ki to Solve Life Problems

Once we decide to take a problem into our own hands, we take the initiative, and expand our mental horizons. But many problems require considerable analysis and effort before they yield up a solution. Looking for a job, entering a marriage, managing a group of unwilling people; some problems are very complex. Often the reason we have difficulty making decisions and solving problems, is a lack of information; insufficient perspective to make and carry out a judgment. The more a problem weighs on us, the narrower our field of vision becomes, ending in a state of mental paralysis.

In order to gain the information and perspective that we need on a problem, we must stimulate the mind with questions. Rather than seeking to fix or avoid the ambiguity of the situation, we should seek to meet it head on and understand it. A simple way to do this is to begin thinking on paper. Making a list; considering possible solutions on paper, can widen your perspective. Ask yourself: "What do I want?", or "What is the real problem?" Don't be satisfied with a small list of answers, and don't reject something because now it seems impractical. Ten or twenty items may still not be enough to yield an answer. When you feel you have exhausted the possibilities, then edit the list. Prepare a new list by selecting several of the best ideas from the old one, or by combining some of those ideas into better ones. This still may not yield an answer, but it will be closer. After taking time away from the problem, expand and condense the same list again, or refine your question by making it more specific. It is as important to condense the list, as it is to expand it. The process is similar to that of deep breathing, in that it takes time to expand the range of your thinking.

It may also be helpful to write out your analysis in journal form, rewriting and editing your first draft until the essence of the problem becomes clear. Whether you make a list, or write a journal, you are gathering information about the problem. When you condense or edit what you have written, you put it in perspective; and determine what is important. By brainstorming on paper, you produce a refined statement of purpose; a statement of direction sufficient to regenerate your life.

You may not yet know what you ultimately want, but you will have taken the initiative toward solving the problem. And you will have increased your capacity to absorb and digest information. When our capacity to digest information is small, we suffer from information overload, one of the symptoms of future shock. Our potential capacity to absorb information is great. But our capacity to organize and make sense of it may be limited. Strong Ki, that is a strong sense of purpose and intent, automatically expands that capacity.

If we are honest with ourselves, sooner or later we encounter our own limits. No one has all of the knowledge and experience to solve every problem, entirely by himself. Some questions cannot be answered by brainstorming alone. Reaching this limit, it is time to go outside of oneself to find the answer. Somewhere, someone has experienced and solved a similar problem. Somewhere, someone has the information or advice that you are seeking. If it isn't in print, it may be in someone's life, or work experience. The only way to find out is to ask. There are many ways of askings; many kinds of research. It only begins in the library. A good reference librarian will overwhelm you with sources of information on any subject, organization, or person that you wish to know more about. The only way to protect yourself against the avalanche of information that you may encounter, is to continually refine your statement of purpose. Focus your mental image of what it is that you want to find out or accomplish.

No wind favors the ship without port of destination. If you don't know where you are going, or what you want in life; then it doesn't really matter what you do. If you are content to rest with the status quo, then you can resign yourself to whatever happens, satisfied that you couldn't do anything about it anyway.

At some point, your research will lead you to talk face to face with other people, who may be able to assist you where you cannot help yourself. By the time information is in print, it is usually already out of date. Many important events never reach print until they are already fixed; when it may be too late to influence them. We naturally hesitate to meet and question people that we do not know. But if your questions are specific enough, if you have done your homework so that you know what you are talking about; if you are open, sincere, and enthusiastic enough in your approach; there are few people who will turn you away without some helpful leads or advice. Since this advice is usually given freely, it should be received with due appreciation, perhaps followed up by a thank-you note, if they gave generously of their time. Some of the books and sources in the bibliography go into great detail about how to do this.

This process of asking and attempting to answer and refine meaningful questions, gradually changes you. It produces a deep and creative discontent. It drives you to overcome the inertia which threatens to stifle the life force within you. Made fully alive by this discontent, the mind becomes very calm; like a rapidly spinning top. It appears still, but it is full of power, full of Ki. The mind which seeks to be left alone and undisturbed, is also still; but it is the stillness of death.

No two people are alike. Each person is a unique combination of experiences and abilities, with limitless potential for development. The reason that most people fail to realize this potential, is that they lack intitiative. Their minds and bodies are disjointed, working at cross purposes. They see themselves as victims of forces beyond their control; and they are perfectly happy to accept laws, advice, and philosophies which reinforce that idea. Though they complain, they rarely avail themselves of opportunities to change.

There was once a young ballet student who loved to dance, but lacked confidence in her potential to pursue it seriously. She needed to make a decision about her future, so she asked her ballet teacher for his honest opinion: did she have the talent to make it as a professional dancer? His answer was, "No. Not a chance." Disappointed, but relieved to know the truth, she gave up dancing, led a very ordinary life, and put on some weight over the years. But somehow she never quite got over ballet, and continued somewhat wistfully to go to concerts. Years later, she accidentally bumped into her former ballet teacher after a concert. She asked him if he remembered her; and told him that, although he had told her that she had no potential as a dancer, she had continued to watch concerts over the years. He replied, "Oh, I tell everyone that. The one's who really have what it takes, pay no attention. They go ahead and do it anyway."

Ki training can strengthen us to accomplish whatever we need and want to do in life. It can give us the initiative to make full use of the resources which lay all about us. It can draw to us the people who can help us, and whom we can help. And it can help us realize the potential that we were born to. If we fail to do this, the responsibility, and the loss, is ours.

13. Increasing Personal and Professional Effectiveness

Doing Things Well

All forms of energy must be focused and harnessed, in order to be useful. Ki is no different. Like wind and water, it is hardly noticed when it is diffuse; but is capable of tremendous power when it is concentrated and directed. Yet we need not wait for a crisis to experience this power in our lives. Nor is it totally beyond our control. The real problem of Ki development is how to bring the transcendent power of Ki into our daily lives, into everything that we do; how to develop our full human potential.

First in life, we need initiative. But we also need particular abilities. We must be able to perform or achieve some things well; not just to earn a living, but to enjoy life. In short, we must develop and focus our Ki.

Everyone develops some skills in life. It requires some skill just to cope with problems, and to survive from day to day. However, most of the skills that we use every day, do little to develop or focus our Ki. This is one reason why there is so little job satisfaction. Anyone can make money. It requires something more to truly make a living. Though many people never discover it, all are born with an innate talent; an in-born aptitude or gift for doing something very well. It may yet be only a mere hobby or pastime. Or it may be underdeveloped from neglect, but everyone is uniquely gifted to do something, better than anyone else can. A person's talents usually come so easily, that they tend to be taken for granted, or undervalued. Skills are acquired; talents are in-born. A skill is something that we do more or less well, or correctly. A talent is a skill which comes naturally and easily.

When a person is truly gifted at something, this talent is an expression of the original unity of mind and body. It shows the freedom of performance without conflict. Because Ki is strongest when we express our natural aptitudes, we usually enjoy what we do best. Those who are lucky enough to discover and cultivate their in-born talents develop a strong sense of purpose and meaning in life. For a fortunate few, this leads to a true vocation, or calling, in the original sense of the word. For such people, mind and body unification is truly a matter of daily practice.

Without some degree of mind and body coordination, it is almost impossible to discover and cultivate one's talents, and employ them in the pursuit of a meaningful career. Few parents, teachers, or managers are enlightened enough to encourage the people in their charge to develop their talents in this way. Social institutions have their own separate agendas, which often shows little regard for the individual. This is ironic, because often it is in the full development and maturity of those abilities, that society itself most benefits. Genius rarely gains wide recognition in its time. Yet its influence invariably outlives those who oppose it. Genius is a birth-right, but it requires strong Ki to pursue it against the inertia of self and society.

Talent is not something acquired at school or learned on the job. Talents are unique combinations of in-born skills. Like fingerprints, no two people's abilities are alike. But they are so much a part of us, that they are sometimes hard to recognize. They become apparent however, when we are engaged in the pursuit of our goals. Meaningful goals enliven, encourage, and inspire a person. A goal is particularly meaningful if a person has the talent necessary to achieve it. How well it is achieved, and how long it takes, depends on the level of mind and body coordination applied to it.

Ki development can help you to recognize your talents. Begin by asking yourself what you like; what you admire. We are inwardly drawn to activities in which we can make use of our talents, though our mental images may be somewhat vague at first. Because talents are with us from an early age, they usually find early ex-pression. A person who picks up foreign languages quickly, was probably a good mimic as a child. Good mechanics were usually working under the hood before they could drive. Our values and ideals also tell us something about our talents. When we are drawn to something, we react strongly to anything which pulls us away from it. The easiest way to recognize our talents, is from the feedback that we get in the pursuit of our goals. If you are good at something, people will tell you in one way or another. They may compliment you or admire your work. You may receive formal recognition. Demands for your time may come in the form of job offers or increased business. Or you may meet resistance at the beginning, from people who don't understand what you are doing. But it is impossible to make sense of any of this feedback without clear goals. Whatever task you undertake, pursue it with mind and body unified, and your goals will become clear. The results of your pursuit depend on your skills and talents. Ki will help you to do anything reasonably well, but some things better than others. If you find that using Ki, you learn very quickly and perform well enough to draw notice from others, then you have probably identified a natural aptitude. If you enjoy it, and find boundless energy to pursue it, then you have probably identified a talent; and you won't need any encouragement to continue. Refine and develop your talent with Ki, and you will achieve something of significant personal or professional value.

Increasing Personal Effectiveness

We have seen how Ki can improve effectiveness in a number of the traditional arts of Japan. Many of these disciplines have been refined for hundreds of years, as techniques of Ki development. Many of the Japanese arts are increasingly available to Western students, both in Japan and overseas. More and more information is breaking the language barrier, and increasing numbers of Western instructors are being trained in Japan. Still, for the vast majority of Westerners, there is no easy access to these arts.

But Ki is not limited to any particular art or culture. It can find expression in any aspect of daily life. Mind and body coordination will increase personal effectiveness in sports, various occupational and professional skills, and in dealing with people. It will make sense of the advice and methods of talented people who have discovered these things on their own. And it will provide a constant reference in developing your skills and talents, professional or otherwise.

All activities involving skill require repetition. Sports players practice the same moves over and over. Machine operators repeat the same actions hour after hour. Office work involves many routines. Even creative work involves repetition and some mechanical tasks. Repetition itself is neither good nor bad. But it does reinforce habits, good and bad. This is why it is essential to work and play with mind and body unified. Careless actions are not only ineffective; they are dangerous. "How-to" books exist on nearly every human activity. While most of these books are written by people who have some ability to perform a skill, it is a rare book that tells how to learn. It is easy to explain how to do something; but another matter to explain how to do it well. Books on baseball explain how to hold the bat, but not how to calm the mind so the the batter can see the ball clearly. Textbooks on surgery explain how to make an incision, but not how to hold the hand with steady control. Books on public speaking tell how to organize and present one's ideas, but not how to genuinely hold an audience with the power of your expression. Books on speed reading offer techniques of skimming large amounts of information, but they don't tell how to think. This is why many things cannot be learned from a book, and people will gladly pay money for lessons, in which they hear the same words that are written in a book. Without feedback from a teacher, it is very difficult to avoid developing bad habits. Years of doing something the wrong way not only destroys your effectiveness at that particular task, but it can result in any number of occupational or recreational diseases. Typists develop chronically stiff shoulders from habitually typing with weight upperside. Drivers and other people who use their arms, experience the same problem. Sports professionals often experience injuries, and are forced to retire from professional play at a relatively young age, because they engage in dynamic or high stress activities without mind and body fully unified. Teachers lose their voices yelling at students. Managers under stress lose their ability to make good judgments. The list is endless. Because human activities involve repetition, and subconscious habits form quickly, it is essential to perform them correctly from the beginning, with mind and body coordination. This is not only the most effective way to work; it is the safest.

A common assumption is that one person can only do so much, or that there are only so many hours in the day. This is based on very limited thinking, which assumes that everyone operates alone, with a limited quota of hours to spend in life. Actually, time and space are quite relative. Our ability to perform, and the limits of what we can accomplish, depend far more on the strength of our Ki, and the amount of help and support we get from the people around us. If you trust in the Universe, and fully coordinate mind and body, then it will supply you with ample energy and resources to accomplish whatever you need and want to do; particularly if it is consistent with the purposes and talents which the Universe has given you. As you help others, so will they help you. Life leads you to an increasing number of mutually beneficial relationships and encounters.

In fact we can do nothing alone. Unification of mind and body is really unification with the Universe, and all that lives within it. The more you realize this process in your daily life, the more it will come to your assistance. Trust in the Universe, extend strong Ki, and you will find help coming from totally unexpected directions. Though the pressure might be great, stress and fear will be small. You will have the support and assistance of people and powers beyond your own limited self.

Gaining Cooperation from Others

One of the best ways to succeed at anything is to help others became successful. Gradually, they will come to recognize the benefits of an alliance with you, and will begin to make efforts in your behalf. Part of recognizing our essential oneness with the Universe, is realizing that without the assistance of others, we are helpless to do anything. The two least reliable ways of getting this assistance, are forcing people to act in your service, or buying their assistance. Both of these ways encourage dependence. They create resentment, because they are motivated by selfish gain, and not mutual cooperation. The most reliable way of getting and keeping the cooperation of others is to help them to help themselves, without demanding that they return in kind. This encourages independence, and offends no one. Giving gifts with strings attached is really a form of coercion. On the other hand, giving something for nothing, in the form of hand-outs, or welfare to the able-bodied, merely stifles initiative. The best gift that you can give, is one that helps another to become stronger and more self-sufficient. This is why the teacher usually learns more and progresses faster than the student. Once you learn how to coordinate mind and body, if you wish to progress, you have an obligation to teach whatever you know to others. Don't be concerned that your knowledge is incomplete. It can only be completed by sharing it with others who aren't as privileged. However, though you can lead them to water, you can't force them to drink it.

Any assistance that you render should be given with Ki; that is without expectation of a fair exchange. Small minds trade favors tit for tat, and always keep score. Once Ki is extended, that Ki goes on forever, and never returns. However, fresh Ki immediately replaces it, from a different direction; so there is no loss, unless you try to get it back. You reap as you sow, but not necessarily in the same form or time. The good that you do returns to you, but you know not how. The same is true of the harm that you do. If you cut yourself off from the Universe, then it too will abandon you in time.

During the Edo period in Japan, a wealthy merchant was said to have donated a large sum of money to the Engaku temple in Kamakura. When he complained to the abbot, because he received not a word of thanks; he was told that the giver should be thankful. All of our gifts are opportunities to enlarge ourselves. By helping others to help themselves, we multiply our friends and allies accordingly. The size or monetary value of the gift is irrelevant. What matters, is that we extend Ki to others when we help them. This can be done without any exchange of material gifts whatsoever. Just believe in and encourage the other person's ability to extend positive Ki, and to help themselves.

Behind any great human achievement, there is always a hidden network of unseen allies and supporters, who have made it possible for that one person to succeed. In medieval Japan, amidst the chaos of many warring states, a nobleman once called his three sons together, to discuss what would happen to the family after he died. He gave each an arrow, and asked him to bend it. All three were easily able to snap their arrow in two. Then he gave each of them three arrows, and asked them to try to break all three at the same time. None could even bend the arrows. After this, he counseled them to maintain their strength through unity after his death. Self-sufficiency is really a misnomer. We only appear to be independent when we are self-sufficient. A better word would be resourceful. Though no one is free from the obligation to work and struggle in life, a resourceful person is never lacking in what he or she wants and truly needs. Help can come in many forms, but it invariably comes through other people.

Personality and the Sources of Human Conflict

If human beings are essentially one with the Universe, and with each other, then why are they always fighting? Why is there so much dissension in the world? Whether with words or with weapons, people spend much of their lives in conflict with other people.

We are in conflict over our differences. When the mind is calm, we can feel our oneness with others through Ki. We can control and direct Ki, but we cannot possess or contain it; because Ki is beyond individual personality. Our differences spring from personality or character. We need not subjugate or eliminate personality to get along, anymore than we need to have the same bodies. Our mind and body are something that we inherit from the Universe through our parents. However, just as a person is more than just a body, so we are more than just our personality. It is at the deeper level, beyond personality, that we are one, and without conflict.

When the mind is rough and unsettled, it can only perceive the differences between people. Completely selfish people are so totally self-absorbed, that they are even unaware of the differences. Without the strength and composure of mind and body unification, these differences are threatening. As a result, there is endless misunderstanding between people. The most common reaction to the differences in character, is to assume that there is something wrong with the other person. Great efforts are made in families, schools, and organizations to mold people into something that they are not. Behavior can be partially controlled by threats and rewards. If the controls are pervasive enough, they can warp the original character. It is a great tragedy to lose the original character; because that is where one's talents and life purpose reside.

The stronger the Ki, the greater the ability to resist efforts to control and distort the character. It is almost impossible to permanently mask this original essence, even biologically. Plastic surgeons may be able to alter a person's face dramatically. But in time, the original character surfaces again in the face, and makes itself known. The faces of youth are less revealing than those of later years, because it takes time for the character to form and express itself in the face. In both the criminal and the genius, there is often a dramatic change between the face of youth, and that of adulthood. Neither make-up not surgery can hide the essence of what is inside. Ultimately, it will out. Its most beautiful form is the one which is unified in character and purpose.

Carl Jung devised a scheme which is useful for understanding differences in character. It is based on four dimensions of the personality: orientation towards other people; orientation towards reality; values in decision making; and degree of desire for closure. There are endless variations and combinations possible within these four dimensions. No combination is good or bad in itself; all have potential for both. Trouble arises when one type tries to change or manipulate another type. Conflicts arise from misunderstanding the differences between people, and trying to force others to be something that they are not (Fig. 13-1).

The first dimension involves orientation towards other people. The two ex-

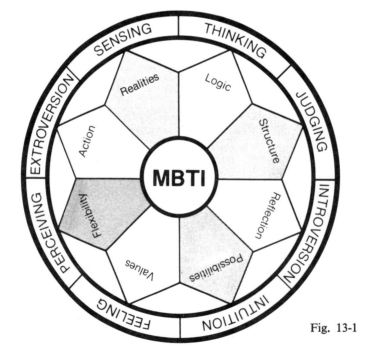

Fig. 13-1

tremes are *Extroversion* and *Introversion*, with most people falling somewhere in between. More precisely, these terms suggest one's orientation toward *Action* or *Reflection*. It has nothing to do with how friendly or self-confident a person may be. Nor is one better than the other. Ki is beyond both of them, and finds easy expression on either end of the scale. Extroverts tend to turn to others under pressure; Introverts tend to seek privacy and internal space. Because of the differences in their response to other people, they tend to misunderstand each other at a superficial level. From a unified posture, they can learn mutual respect.

The second dimension of character involves orientation towards reality. Some people are *Sensing* oriented; others see things *Intuitively*. Sensing types focus on reality, facts, and what they can see. Intuitive people see things in terms of possibilities. Both are valid ways of viewing the world. Sometimes the meaning is in the print; sometimes it is between the lines. Whether seeing things as they are, or as they could be, one's perception will be far more accurate if the mind is calm and alert. However, because perception is the basis of one's orientation to reality, differences in this dimension can lead to major misunderstandings between people. Everyone is capable of both ways of viewing the world, but we habitually rely on one faculty more than the other. Both faculties are skills, which are rooted in the personality. It is very helpful if we can learn to respect other ways of seeing the world. Ki is beyond both sensation and intuition. It can serve as the basis for unity where personalities clash.

The third dimension has to do with values in decision making. At one extreme, decisions and interpretations are made impersonally, in terms of *Thinking* and *Logic*. At the other extreme, decisions and interpretations are made personally, in terms of *Feeling* and *Values*. Most people tend to feel that one is better than the other. This reflects a relative character preference, not an absolute value. Both can be humane; either can be cruel. Whichever our character tendency, we should learn to use the faculty, and not be used by it. We rarely have enough information to make a wise decision alone. Other people can help, but their perception and values are limited too. Ki meditation can help calm and sharpen the mind to the point where it can make reliable judgments and decisions in any situation. It can also reveal the value in other peoples' perspective on a problem.

The fourth dimension of character is the degree of desire for closure. This too is neutral; neither good nor bad, except in the degree to which it is anchored in mind and body unity. At one extreme is the faculty of *Judging*, which has a strong desire to achieve closure through structure. At the other extreme is the desire to avoid closure, by *Perceiving* and keeping options flexible and fluid. Whichever one's orientation, one is likely to feel a sense of resistance when dealing with people of the opposite orientation. Both attitudes have advantages and disadvantages; neither is fundamentally better than the other. Calming the mind can help you to see why a person of the opposite orientation thinks and acts the way he does. Though this need not change your own opinion, it can improve communication and help obtain cooperation from others.

It is possible to analyze these differences extensively, and detailed studies have been made on the varieties of character that emerge from various combinations.

For example, a person who is an *Introverted, Intuitive, Thinking, Judging* type, may have a keen sense for the possibilities of translating theory into substance, yet may not be so concerned with conventional ways of doing things. An *Extroverted, Intuitive, Feeling, Perceiving* type may have the ability to generate lots of enthusiasm for new projects, yet may suffer from muscle tension and over-excitement. An *Extroverted, Sensing, Thinking, Perceiving* type may have a dramatic flair and a marvelous sense of humor, yet might be insensitive to others' feelings. Not only are different combinations possible, but different degrees exist within each orientation; leading to the endless variety that makes up the human family. Furthermore, a person's character may or may not mature and develop according to its original essence. The character, like the body, can become sick and distorted, or it can grow strong and healthy. The choice is ours.

As important as character differences are, it is best not to dwell too extensively on them in relations with other people, particularly with groups of people. Acknowledge them; don't try to force people to be what they are not. If you coordinate mind and body well in daily life, then your character will mature naturally. As mind and body grow stronger, your talents will emerge, and you will discover a new sense of direction and purpose in life. This is known as living in harmony with the Universe. Your direction may or may not be in harmony with the people around you at a given time; but if you proceed with conviction, you will find the resources and alliances that you need to fulfill your purpose.

Self-Mastery is the Key to Leadership

As no two people are alike in personality, there is always the potential for conflict. Usually this conflict is kept within socially acceptable bounds. When it gets out of control, it breeds crime and poverty, and in extreme cases, war. Most people never go beyond the personality level. In order to gain cooperation and respect from others, they are forced to make use of manipulative psychological techniques, variations on the carrot or the stick. These techniques do modify behavior, but they also create resistance in the personality, because they show no respect for character integrity.

Ultimately, it is more effective to speak and relate to people on a deeper level than personality, with Ki. This shows respect for character differences, and at the same time acknowledges the underlying unity with the other person. The combination is irresistible. Showing respect and understanding for the other person's way of relating to people, viewing reality, making decisions, and attitude towards closure, we occasion no resistance in the personality, despite our differences. If the other person knows that we accept and respect them as they are, they will be more willing to listen to what we have to say. If we speak with Ki, our words will have much greater impact. This is true whether we ask for help, offer advice and constructive criticism, or express affection. People will recognize your sincerity, and know that it is genuine. And despite your differences, they will do their best to help you, or at least not interfere.

There may however be some people with strong vested interests in preventing you from being yourself, or from developing your talents. It is not possible to win over everyone to your side. You may need strong Ki to overcome their resistance, but don't fight their personality. Maintain mind and body coordination, despite the added stress of personal conflict, and with luck, you will win the respect of your opponents in the end.

The key to real leadership then, is self-mastery. A master horseman leads the horse from the One Point, creating no resistance to his lead. The horse willingly goes where he is lead, hardly conscious of the rider. Beginners pull with the arms and force too much, hurting the horse's mouth and irritating the animal. Similarly, a good horse need never taste the whip. It can feel its master's lead at the slightest touch. A dull animal won't move until it feels the sting of the whip or spur. The horse and rider are not different from many human relationships, particularly those involving leaders and followers: parents, teachers, managers. Most organizations are rife with tension and conflict, because the leaders and followers are always at cross-purposes. Parents don't understand their children, teachers have no respect from their students; management and labor communicate through lawyers. Caught up in their differences, they find no mutual respect or common ground. Ki development teaches us that our true master is the Universe itself. It guides and trains us through our life experience, if we but let it.

As we gain self-mastery, we begin to take the lead, rather than just respond to it. A fortunate few come to realize that mind and body, rider and horse, are inseparable; a dynamic expression of the pulse of Universal Life.

天
人
工
拙

Real talents are in-born.
Do not look to others to find them.
—Chuang Tzu
(Translation and *tenkoku* seal carving by author.)

Bibliography and Sources of Further Information

By way of reference, there are dozens of books available on Japanese culture. But books have an inherent limitation: they cannot provide you with feedback on your own learning progress. Also needed is personal instruction. Sources of further information and instruction follow, organized by topic.

KI, AIKIDŌ, and KIATSU

KI NO KENKYÛKAI HQ
101   Ushigome Heim, 2–30 Haramachi
Shinjuku, Tokyo
Tel: (03) 353–3461, 3461

International Branches of the KI NO KENKYÛKAI:

Please note that not all of these are actual *dojo* addresses.

USA

HAWAII
Honolulu Ki Society
2003 Nuuanu Ave.
Honolulu, HI 96817

Big Island Aikido-Ki Club
P.O. Box 438
Papakou, HI 96781

Maui Aikido-Ki Society
P.O. Box 724 Wailuku
Maui, HI 96793

Kaui Ki Society
2901 Pua Loke St. Lihue
Kauai, HI 96766

CALIFORNIA
Northern California Ki Society
  Federation
130 Willits St.
Daly City, CA 94014

Southern California Ki Society
P.O. Box 3752
Gardena, CA 90247

NORTHEAST
Northwest Ki Society
P.O. Box 02025
Portland, OR 97202

Seattle Ki Society
6106 Roosevelt Way NE.
Seattle, WA 98115

MIDLAND
Midland Ki Society Federation
P.O. Box 818
Boulder, CO 80306

Chicago Ki Society
7721 S. Luella
Chicago, IL 60649

Arizona Ki Society
8306 East Welsh Trail
Scottsdale, AZ 85258

EAST COAST
Virginia Ki Society
5631 Cornish Way
Alexandria, VA 22310

Montgomery County Ki-Aikido Society
19004 Rolling Acres Way
Olney, MD 20832

New Jersey Ki Society
529 Howard Street
Riverton, NJ 08077

South Carolina Ki Society
Department of Philosophy
Furman University
Greenville, SC 29613

Others:

AUSTRALIA
Australian Ki Society
6 Nurran St.
Mount Gravatt
Brisbane, 4122

NEW ZEALAND
New Zealand Ki Society
P.O. Box 1140
Auckland

SINGAPORE
Ki no Kenkyû Kai-Singapore Branch
53 Paterson Road
Singapore 0923

PHILIPPINES
Ki Society of the Philippines
90 Women's Club Street Santol
Quezon City 1113

CONTINENTAL EUROPE
AND UNITED KINGDOM
European Ki Society
19 Rue De La Cité
1050 Bruxelles
Belgium

The Ki Society HQ in Tokyo also sponsors an intensive two-year training and certification program for Aikidô instructors and another for Kiatsu therapists, beginning each April. Write to them directly in English, for further information.

Recommended books on Ki include —————————————————————

Ki in Daily Life, by Koichi Tohei, Ki-no-Kenkyûkai, 1980.
Book of Ki: Coordinating Mind and Body in Daily Life, by Koichi Tohei, Japan Publications, Inc., 1976.
Kiatsu, by Koichi Tohei, Ki-no-Kenkyûkai, 1983.
Aikidô with Ki, by Koretoshi Maruyama, Ki-no-Kenkyûkai, 1984.

SHODŌ:

Hundreds of schools exist in Japan for the study of calligraphy. For information, please write:

> Reed Research Institute
> Tada Bldg. 402
> 1–9–5 Ebisu
> Shibuya-ku, Tokyo 150, Japan
> Tel: 03–473–2108

THE GAME OF GO:

Japan: Nihon Ki-in
7–2 Gobancho
Chiyoda-ku, Tokyo, 102
USA: American Go Association
P.O. Box 379, Old Chelsea Station
New York, NY 10011
United Kingdom: British Go Association
60 Wantage Road
Reading, Berks. PG3 2SF
F. R. Germany: Deutscher Go Bund
Ahornstrasse 12
8032 Locham bei Munchen

Recommended readings

Go for Beginners, by Kaoru Iwamoto, Penguin Books, 1976
Basic Techniques of Go, by Isamu Haruyama, The Ishi Press, 1969
Strategic Concepts of Go, by Yoshiaki Nagahara, The Ishi Press, 1972

NOH DRAMA:

> Mr. Richard Emmert
> Noh Research Archives
> Musashino Joshi Daigaku
> Shinmachi 1–1–20
> Hoya-shi, Tokyo 202 Japan

Recommended reading is *On the Art of the Noh Drama: the Major Treatises of Zeami*, translated by J. Thomas Rimer and Masakazu Yamazaki, Princeton University Press, 1984.
The Noh Theater: Principles and Perspectives, by Kunio Komparu, John Weatherhill, Inc., 1983.

TEA CEREMONY: ━━━━━━━━━━━━━━━━━━━━━━━━━━━━

Urasenke Foundation
Ogawa Teranouchi
Agaru, Kamikyo-ku,
Kyoto, Japan 602

Urasenke Cha-no-Yu Center
153 East 69th St.
New York, NY 10021

Tea Ceremony Society of Urasenke
866 United Nations Plaza, Room 451
New York, NY 10017

Recommended reading includes ━━━━━━━━━━━━━━━━━━━━━━━━━━━━

Chadô: The Japanese Way of Tea, by Sen no Soshitsu, John Weatherhill, Inc.,
　Tokyo, 1979.
The Way of Tea, by Rand Castile, John Weatherhill, Inc., Tokyo.

Career and Character Development ━━━━━━━━━━━━━━━━━━━━━━━━━

Hal and Marilyn Shook
Life Management Services, Inc.
6825 Redmond Deive
McLean, Virginia 22101 USA
Tel: 703–356–2630

I personally recommend Hal and Marilyn Shook, and their seminars in Career
and Life Planning, Management Development, and Client Relations. They are
personable and professional, and are familiar with Ki Development.

Recommended readings includes ━━━━━━━━━━━━━━━━━━━━━━━━━━

What Color is Your Parachute?, by Richard Nelson Bolles, published annually
　by the Ten Speed Press.
Please Understand Me: Character and Temperament Types, by David Kearsey and
　Marilyn Bates, Prometheus Nemesis Book Co., 1984. This book is available,
　along with other Jung-related materials, including decales and posters of the
　mandala on personality types appearing in this book, from:
　　　　　Eleanor Corlett
　　　　　Consultant on the Myers-Briggs Type Indicator
　　　　　205 Tapawingo Rd., S. W.
　　　　　Vienna, Virginia 22180 USA

A Word on Studying in Japan:

An increasing number of foreigners are finding it easy to live in Japan for a period of months or years, support oneself teaching English, and pursue an in-depth study of Ki or Ki-related arts. Many come with idealized preconceptions about Japan, and about Japanese teachers. Japan is a mecca for the study of Ki; but it is also a modern nation, and most of the people know very little about the Ki principles presented in this book. The *Sensei*, or teacher who has mastered it, is also a person. Foreigners should come to Japan with an open mind, realizing that the Japanese are human, and that they have their own way of doing things, which may not fit Western ideals of what they should be. Yet herein lies the value of study in Japan. One can learn first-hand that to master Ki does not require you to give up your personality, or suppress your individuality. On the contrary, it develops it. The language is a barrier, but not to the study of Ki or the arts. Many foreigners gain great benefit from their study here, without ever learning to speak a word of Japanese. However, judgment of the Japanese people, and their way of doing things, should at least be reserved until you have mastered the language, or lived in Japan for at least a year.

Recommended reading for those who wish to study in Japan includes ————

Japan: A Travel Survival Kit, by Ian Mcqueen, Lonely Planet Press.
Jobs in Japan, by John Wharton, The Global Press, Denver, 1983.

> Reed Research Institute
> Tada Bldg. 402
> 1–9–5 Ebisu
> Shibuya-ku, Tokyo 150, Japan
> Tel: 03–473–2108

Index